Iona,

Thank you for
Constanting inspiring me!

♡ Jessica

DEDICATION

For my grandma.

To my niece and nephews: I hope that you each have your own adventures.

And for G, for letting me be your copilot.

AUTHOR'S NOTE

To write this book, I relied upon my personal journals, e-mails, and memories. I have changed some of the names of individuals and organizations—but not all—to preserve privacy. I write my experiences from a purely personal standpoint. From what I've gathered from other travelers, my experiences are unusual when compared to those of others who have worked abroad in New Zealand. I would highly recommend everyone goes to New Zealand to experience their own adventure.

In addition, I practice a form of Buddhism that involves chanting "Nam Myoho Renge Kyo." I mention this throughout the book because it is inextricable from my life; it is a part of my story. I'm grateful that my Buddhist practice provides me with a built-in community of absolutely amazing people wherever I go.

ACKNOWLEDGMENTS

Cyan Corwine, thank you for laughing and crying with me and for our pinky promise. I'd like to thank Liam and Olivia for kindly proofreading my book. Special thanks to Thomas Sainsbury and Roberto Nascimento for laughing at me and with me. Jim and Vicky, thank you for being the best neighbors a Buddhist girl could have. Natalie, thank you for taking me under your wing. Thank you to Katie, Andrew Mockler, Colin Mathura-Jeffree, Steve Wrigley, Phill, Anna, Shaunna, Lynda, Joan, Kana, Liam, Bjorn, Lulu, Marie, and the lovely people I met in New Zealand and Samoa for all being in my life. Thank you to the beautiful country of New Zealand, which allowed me to call it home for a bit.

I'd also like to express immense gratitude for having the worst bosses in both California and New Zealand. You taught me how to value myself and believe in my talents when no one else did. I'd also like to thank the character I refer to as Gretchen in the book: I hope that if you read this you're able to laugh with me and that you're healthy and well. Thank you to all of my teachers, who have come in the most fascinating forms.

Lastly, thank you to my parents and stepparents for trusting in my leap of faith.

TUESDAY, JULY 6, 2010

I landed in the dark, with one suitcase, a backpack, and a pillow. I have what I need and nothing more. The work-abroad company I got a holiday working visa through instructed me to get on a bus, which took me to Ace Hostel in the Auckland city center. I'd never been out of the country for longer than ten days before, and this was my first time traveling alone.

It was still dark when I got to the hostel. Jet-lagged, I fell asleep quickly and didn't wake up until the next day. There is a young French-Canadian girl who just arrived and is jet-lagged too. She slept in the bunk above me. In the middle of my long sleep, a very tall person with shaggy hair came into the room and slept in the bunk across from mine. I thought, "That is one ugly girl." In the morning, I realized it was a guy. I didn't know the hostel rooms were unisex. Without my contact lenses in, I squinted at him from my sleeping bag, "Are you a guy?"

In the morning, I opened the curtains to my hostel room. The window faced a brick wall. I almost burst into tears.

At the airport in San Francisco, my suitcase was nearly twice the weight limit. The airline gave me a giant plastic bag that I frantically filled with heavy things, like my winter boots and the Lonely Planet New Zealand tour book, then I handed it to my worried mom telling her, "I guess I'll figure it out when I get there."

From my window in a hostel, I have a view of a brick wall. I have no plans, no expectations. I just needed to go.

I managed to skim a tour book before leaving. The book said, "New Zealand is one of the safest countries in the world. New Zealand's population has a hundred thousand fewer men than women." It also advised to wear sunscreen and not drink pond water or walk in dark alleys late at night.

Last October, I decided to boycott dating after having my heart broken so badly that I felt like a raw skinned animal. New Zealand seemed like the perfect place to avoid the opposite sex and have some much needed alone time. I'd been dating since I was thirteen years old. At twenty-six, I've spent half my life dating and haven't had a minute to myself.

I'm going cold turkey with guys. No dating for one year.

WEDNESDAY, JULY 7, 2010

I'm officially the oldest person in the hostel. There's a nice English girl named Marie who's now sharing my hostel room. We went to the grocery store together. The chips— or crisps, as Marie calls them—come in weird flavors I've never seen before, like lamb and mint. The money in New Zealand is rainbow colored and has pictures of ferns, penguins and other birds, mountaineers, and the queen of England. The dollar is a golden coin with the kiwi bird on it. My favorite coin is the ten-cent piece with a Maori carving. The ten-cent coin is also the smallest. Everything

2

is just rounded up or down at the registers.

Marie and I made pasta in the hostel kitchen together tonight. The pots and pans looked dirty and rusted. About thirty people were all cooking different meals at the same time. Everyone looks to be in their late teens or early twenties and trying to figure out how to cook. The smell of food combined with smoke from food burning in filthy pots and pans made me gag.

As Marie and I ate our pasta, a nineteen-year-old English boy sat next to us. He looked at me strangely and asked how old I was. When I responded twenty-six, his eyes almost popped out of his head, and he said, "Wow! You're the oldest person here!"

THURSDAY, JULY 8, 2010

I took a bus to the Auckland Domain with a German girl I met at the hostel. At the bus stops are electronic boards that show when the next bus will arrive. Our bus was running two minutes late. The German girl said, "I don't understand, where is the bus?"

"It's late."

"How? Where is it? I don't understand how that is possible."

"What difference does it make?"

"Two minutes," the German girl said very seriously.

On the bus I met a little, old, American lady traveling around New Zealand and couch surfing. I hope I'm a couch-surfing granny when I get old.

I walked around the Auckland Domain with the German girl. She told me, "It's strange to see people walking or sitting on the grass. In Germany, nature is just for looking at."

SUNDAY, JULY 11, 2010

The sexual-energy volume is on mute in Auckland. Walking down Queen Street, the busiest street in the biggest city in the country, all the guys are wearing scarves and don't make eye contact. I feel invisible for the first time since I grew boobs. No one looks at me. It's like I'm in another dimension.

I grew accustomed to getting harassed everywhere I went in California: school, work, walking down the street, or going for a run at Spring Lake in Santa Rosa. It didn't matter what I did or how I dressed, guys in California were like dogs in heat. Once a guy asking me out followed me for blocks. I didn't know what to do, so I pretended I didn't speak English and told him, "No habla Ingles," over and over. After a few blocks, he said, "I'll learn Spanish!" He eventually stopped following me.

In Auckland, even the construction workers don't whistle. I stopped at a construction site and stared at a group of beefy-looking workers with tattoos covering their arms and wearing hard hats and orange vests. I gawked at them in the same way one would stare at an animal at the zoo. They just looked down at their shoes.

MONDAY, JULY 12, 2010

Before I flew solo to New Zealand, I spent a month in Samoa with my aunt who works as a doctor on the island. Her house is directly across the street from the beach with the best snorkeling on the island. I volunteered at the art museum on the island and helped save ancient artifacts from being destroyed by termites and humidity.

I'm feeling extra buoyant due to my Samoan diet of piña coladas, beer, coconuts, hamburgers and fries, and homemade ice cream. Every time I ordered a salad, it had something fried on top or had a thick, creamy dressing. My extra buoyancy helped me snorkel; I barely walked for a month because I mostly floated all day. Floating is not exactly a cardio work out. I'm surprised I don't have a permanent imprint of a snorkel mask on my face. It feels shocking to be in winter in New Zealand and to have to wear shoes, jackets, and jeans again.

TUESDAY, JULY 13, 2010

Maori words are on public signs. I've see people with full facial tattoos and in suits walking down the street to work.

WEDNESDAY, JULY 14, 2010

Growing up in America, I learned ABCs that ended with Z, pronounced Zee. In New Zealand, Z is Zed. The one and only time I heard Zed before traveling was in Pulp Fiction when Bruce Willis's character explains to his girl that they're riding Zed's chopper, and "Zed's dead, baby. Zed's dead."

When I arrived, I got an orientation in the Global Work Abroad Network office where we were given information about New Zealand, "A through Zed." They told us about different options while working aboard. My visa only allows me to work temporary positions. Some other participants have picked kiwi fruit or worked on farms for accommodations.

In the hostel, I told the German girl, "We don't say Zed in America; we say Z."

"What is Z?"

"Z is Zed."

"What? If go to America I am going to have to learn whole new set of English?"

She was using all sorts of Kiwi slang, like "knickers" instead of "underwear," "heaps" for "a lot," and "sweet as."

"Yes, some of the things you say I had never heard of before I came to New Zealand. If you go to America and say the Kiwi slang with your German accent, Americans might think you're saying German words, and then they will go to Germany and start speaking Kiwi."

THURSDAY, JULY 15, 2010

There's a guy from Texas at the hostel. He told me, "Last night I went to a pub and drank a few beers. I had to walk down a hill to get back to the hostel, and I was like 'Whoa!'" He put out his hands like he was surfing. "I've never walked down a hill before when I was drunk."

"I hear Texas is really flat."

"It is. I've never walked on hills like this before."

"You probably shouldn't tell anyone else that."

SUNDAY, JULY 18, 2010

I found a used condom in the shower at the hostel. I really need to find somewhere else to live.

MONDAY, JULY 19, 2010

Matador Temp Agency interviewed me today. After completing a series of tests on an outdated computer, I was questioned about my resume. A woman not much older than me and wearing a tight skirt and too much makeup sat across the table. With my resume in hand, she

7

looked up at me and asked, "What did you do as a chocolate artist?" She gestured with her hands in a circle and said, "Did you arrange it on platters?"

The word chocolate is not on my resume. I went to San Diego State University, where I studied art and art history. My first job after I graduated was working as a chalkboard artist for a fancy grocery store called Health Nuts.

I looked back at her puzzled. I had an easier time getting around Costa Rica and Peru without knowing more than, "Donde esta el bano?" ("Where is the bathroom?") than I did in New Zealand, where we were theoretically speaking the same language. The people who live in New Zealand are called Kiwis. Kiwis are also a flightless bird and a fruit. The Kiwi accent is like nothing I have ever heard before. They end their sentences in an upward tone, so it always sounds like they are asking a question or singing while mumbling. The vowels are all mixed up. E is I, I is U, and ER sounds like A. "Yes" is "Yis," "Chip" is "Chup," and "Peter" and "Beer" are "Peta" and "Bea."

"Chalkboard," I said to her, praying they use that word

here. Everything has a different word in New Zealand. "Elevator" is now "lift," "garbage" is "rubbish," "cookies" are "biscuits," "to call" is "to ring," "fries" are "chips" and "chips" are "crisps," "sweater" is "jumper," "pissed" isn't "angry" but "drunk," "crazy" is "mad," "apartment" is "flat," "roommate" is "flatmate," and "resume" is "CV."

"Chocolate?"

"Chalkboard. I was a chalkboard artist."

"Chocolate?"

"Chalkboard."

"Chocolate."

Slowly and loudly, I said,
"Chhhhhhaaaaaalllllkkkkkkkkbbbbbbbbboooooooooaaaaaarr
rrrrrddddddddddd!"

As I enunciated, I gestured with my hands as if I were
drawing on a chalkboard in front of me. Maybe sign
language would be more effective, as a blank stare was my
only response.

She looked down at my resume, again studying it with
furrowed brows, and then down at my feet placed in my
teal shoes, "You're going to want to get some black
pumps."

With no more questions, she stood up and walked out of
the room in her generic black pumps, stating, "I am going
to hand over your CV to my colleague. You can wait at
reception."

I anxiously sat on a gray suede couch in the sterile office,
wondering if I had made a mistake coming to this country.
Another woman called my name and took me into a
nearby room.

"I see you volunteered at the museum in Samoa. There's a

position opening up doing data entry in a basement. Does that appeal to you?"

"Sure, that sounds fine," I sighed. Relief swept over me; the job sounded painfully boring, but at least I wouldn't have to talk to people.

TUESDAY, JULY 20, 2010

I'm on the verge of tears while sitting in my cubicle at my new job doing data entry in a basement office at Council. I can't understand anyone's accents, and they can't understand me either. I tell people I came to New Zealand for an adventure living abroad, and now I'm doing data entry in a cubicle. I'd never been in a cubicle before I came to New Zealand. Everyone wears black, white, and gray. I hate how gray the walls are and how boring my job is.

Between October and May, I received three final warnings at my job in California at Health Nuts, an overpriced grocery store. I managed to squirm my way out of all three. Aside from the chalkboard art, I also managed the floral department. But I was complacent and not challenging myself. I've noticed that whenever I'm in a situation like this, not valuing myself or my talent, the universe has a way of kicking my ass out of it. I'm too complacent to leave otherwise. Most of the warnings were bullshit, like for dead flowers on my floral set on my days off, or picking out the wrong vases for Valentine's Day. By May it had got to the point where I either quit or I get fired.

Back then I had one major regret: not living abroad. I had

let the opportunity slip by me in the past because I worried how it would affect the relationship I was in. After spending the last few years constantly getting dumped and only attracting total freaks, and the past few months almost losing my job, I suddenly felt very free—more liberated than I ever felt in my entire life. I realized I was free. I was free to do whatever I wanted—I had no man, no kids, soon no job, and my place was month to month. I had a free place to stay in Samoa and a great recommendation for a work-abroad program. I knew I had to do it all right then because these opportunities would never happen again. In four years I hadn't taken any vacation time so I cashed it all in at once to pay for my flights. It had never dawned on me that I could go on a vacation by myself. This was more than a vacation. It was my great escape. The sun shone the day I was forced to make my decision at Health Nuts. About five minutes after a store manager screamed in my face telling me I had until the end of the day to take the final warning or step down from my position, it started raining while it was still sunny. There was a giant rainbow in the west. Samoa and New Zealand are west of California. I took it as a sign to go—to jump in face first. Within a few weeks, I disassembled my life and was on a plane.

WEDNESDAY, JULY 21, 2010

There's a woman about to go on maternity leave sitting next to me in the office. As she rubs her swollen belly, everyone in the office comes around and tells her birthing stories. The other day at lunch, I almost fainted. A man who always seems maniacally happy said, "It is just

11

amazing how elastic they are! My wife's got bright red and the size of a football!" Ever since then, I have been having lunch by myself behind the building.

THURSDAY, JULY 22, 2010

I took a bus to Remuera to look at a room for rent. On the bus I had to show the driver the printout of where I want to go because he couldn't understand me, and he just told me to sit down. I ended up finding the house, where a strange, lumpy, middle-aged man showed me a lumpy bed on the floor. I definitely don't want to live with him.

MONDAY, JULY 26, 2010

I am aware that I probably have a dirtier mind than the average girl, but everything here in New Zealand sounds like a dirty joke. Nature is called "the bush."

I have been told by Kiwis who are going hiking in the woods, "We're going to the bush."

Hiking is called tramping, so it would be normal for a Kiwi to say, "I went tramping in the bush over the weekend."

One of my coworkers, Natalie, is having a deck built at her house. Since the Kiwi accent pronounces E like an I, when she says, "deck," it sounds like "dick." There has been a lot of discussion about the building of the deck. I tried not to laugh when she was telling me about her deck. She said what sounded like, "It's not nice weather for a dick. The dick should be nice in the summertime."

SATURDAY, JULY 31, 2010

Everything in New Zealand is done through the website Trademe.co.nz. I think it's New Zealand's Craigslist. I looked at a really weird room to rent through Trademe. It was a big Victorian house with all the bedrooms rented out. A middle-aged man in a trench coat opened the door. He looked too excited to meet me and smiled maniacally. He needed a shave and looked like he didn't shower regularly or have any responsibilities.

The front door led into a long hallway. There was a little old man in striped pajamas hunched over and walking down the hallway in the middle of the afternoon. He looked like he was lost or had escaped from an old-folk's home. The man in the trench coat told me the little old man worked nights and slept during the day.

I really need to make a retirement account so that I don't have to live in weird places with weird people when I'm old.

The man in the trench coat showed me the room that was for rent. He told me, "You're destined to live here. Everyone that has rented this room has been named Jamie. You'll be the fifth Jamie."

The current Jamie who rented the room was sitting on her bed, which was placed on a wooden platform sticking out of the wall. There was a ladder for climbing in and out of bed propped against the platform. There weren't any railings on the platform. The only thing preventing her from falling off the platform at night was a car tire.

The other Jamie looked like she was in her late teens or early twenties. I wondered if her parents knew where she was. She waved at me and smiled, "Hi Jamie, nice to meet you. I'm Jamie."

The kitchen had an orange extension cord with a light bulb flung over a chandelier. Sounding proud, the man in the trench coat said, "We had a party, and the light blew. We fixed it, though. Good work, huh? Want a cup of tea?"

"No thank you."

You've got the wrong Jamie; this Jamie is going to stay in the hostel a bit longer.

SUNDAY, AUGUST 1, 2010

I looked at an amazing house today. It was beautiful, like a home you would see in Better Homes and Gardens. It had hardwood floors and a big garden. The landlady renting the room lived there too. She said tenants weren't allowed to do their own laundry; she has to do it. I feel weird about a stranger cleaning my underwear. I guess I'll have to keep looking for a place to live.

SATURDAY, AUGUST 7, 2010

A friend of mine in California worked as a teacher in Japan for a year with a girl from New Zealand named Emily. I got in touch with Emily, and she showed me around. In Piha, she took me to an absolutely beautiful beach with black sand. It doesn't take long to get out of the city. Within a thirty-minute drive, you're in the jungle at the beach. New Zealand is very tropical; the mountains are covered in fern trees.

I expect to see dinosaurs in the jungle here. There's such a feeling of newness, as if it has just emerged from the sea. It feels like anything is possible here. It's such a relief to be anonymous—to have a fresh start, for people to see me for me instead of the rumors they've heard.

I told Emily about my time in Samoa and how I missed it there and thanked her for bringing me to the beach. I really haven't figured out where I am or what I'm doing here. I started crying, and she patted me on the back, "You're still on an island, just a bigger one."

She also took me to the museum, where we watched a traditional Maori performance, and after, Emily said, "There. Now you have been officially welcomed to New Zealand."

TUESDAY, AUGUST 10, 2010

Emily had a friend who was renting her bedroom out while she went home from her university for winter break.

15

I rolled my suitcase from the hostel to the apartment before work over the weekend and moved in. I can see my breath inside the apartment. I thought this was unusual. I told my cubicle coworkers this, and they just rolled their eyes and told me, "Put on another jumper."

I'm sleeping on a single mattress on the ground in my sleeping bag. All the springs in the mattress poke my back. It's weird to live alone in a foreign country. I lived alone in California, but here it feels lonelier. I feel like Goldilocks sleeping in someone else's bed.

My bed at home is enormous. I bought a queen-size bed out of optimism but was always alone. I would sleep sideways it was so big. I was so used to rolling around in my giant bed by myself that, when I got to Samoa, I slept in a single bed and fell out of it while rolling around in my sleep the first week.

Now I'm shivering in my sleeping bag on a mattress (with springs poking me in the back) on the floor while watching my breath. Apparently insulation and heating aren't the norm in houses in New Zealand. There aren't screens on windows or garbage disposals in sinks either. If houses have washing machines, they usually don't have dryers. Everyone dries their clothes on racks they call "clothes horses." It's summer in California. All my friends at home are posting pictures of themselves at the beach on Facebook. I'll give New Zealand one more month before I give up and go home.

16

FRIDAY, AUGUST 13, 2010

Is the gravity different down here? Obviously New
Zealand is at the bottom of the Earth; you can't get much
farther south before you reach Antarctica. Does the
gravitational pull change down here in the way that the
water in the toilets spins the other way?

I keep falling down. After my first week of work doing
data entry in a cubicle, I was walking home and slipped.
My feet flew up in the air, and I landed on my ass. I was
going down a hill and ended up sliding down the hill on
my ass. A lady walking in front of me jumped out of the
way. I almost took her out like a bowling pin.

MONDAY, AUGUST 16, 2010

Today is my birthday. I'm twenty-seven. The pregnant lady
who sits next to me at work bought me a cupcake. It's
strange to have my birthday in the winter. It's been raining
nonstop for the past few weeks.

Last year my birthday sucked. I had to be a bridesmaid in
two weddings, and both the brides-to-be called me about
wedding planning on my birthday, but both forgot to wish
me a happy birthday.

I was very single for both weddings. One of the brides said
she would put me down for two and leave room at the
table for my date because she insisted I bring a date to her
wedding. I begged her, "I'm not bringing a date, please just
put me down for chicken."

17

At her wedding, the rabbi marrying her was also a gynecologist and training to be a psychic. Once the bride called me after a psychic session with her rabbi, "There's a nun in my aura. That's why I don't want to convert."

We had a huge fight because I refused to be a backup dancer in her first dance at the wedding. She wanted me to drive two hours each way, once a week, to attend choreographed, backup dance lessons for her first dance. I hate dancing. I have absolutely no rhythm. The thought of having to dance in front of 350 wedding guests horrified me. The bride insisted, "You're the only bridesmaid that's single, so you're the only one that has time for backup dancing lessons."

All the other bridesmaids were also engaged and were all in each other's weddings. They all talked about wedding details nonstop. I was never the type of girl who fantasized about weddings. I just don't care about stationery, place settings, or dress fittings. I don't know the names of different cuts of diamonds or necklines of dresses.

For a brief moment, I was engaged to my high-school sweetheart. I suggested we have a potluck on the beach. He was insulted by the idea. I just don't see the point in spending a year's salary on one day. I would rather buy a house and get married in my backyard or go on a trip around the world with my husband. After watching the movie Braveheart, I liked the idea of getting married alone in the woods—only me and my husband. I told the other bridesmaids, "I think I just want a Braveheart-style wedding, alone in the woods with my husband, except for the getting raped by the English part."

At one of the bachelorette parties, I was growing weary of hearing about the endless details of weddings. It was a tame party—we just went out for pizza. When the pizza restaurant found out it was a bachelorette party, they brought us over a complimentary pitcher of margaritas in a fishbowl-sized glass with a straw for each girl.

I suggested a chugging contest. There were only five of us girls: me, the two brides-to-be, the maid of honor/designated driver for the evening, and one other bridesmaid.

Both brides-to-be rarely drank and became easily drunk. I knew if I could get them drunk fast it would stop the wedding chatter. I would say chug and pretend to drink as I barely sipped from the top. The two brides-to-be were easily fooled, actually chugging. Their straws were hitting the bottom, where all the alcohol was settling. My plan worked; the brides became too drunk to talk about wedding details and became capable of talking about something—anything—else.

WEDNESDAY, AUGUST 18, 2010

The flat I've been living in started flooding. Part of the roof has collapsed, and water is running down the walls. Every morning when I wake up and turn on the light, the circuit breaker blows. The landlady didn't seem concerned when I called. She said, "It's not an emergency; your life isn't in danger."

19

THURSDAY, AUGUST 19, 2010

Sometimes I carry folders or paperwork and walk aimlessly throughout the office. It's funny to see what people do in their cubicles. I've seen a lot of scrapbook making in the office. You hear a lot of talk about TV shows and sports. Sometimes I see people sleeping while sitting up. Lots of people play solitaire and other crappy computer games or are sneaking on to Facebook. Others are just staring at the clock on the wall, looking like they're about to cry because it isn't five o'clock yet.

FRIDAY, AUGUST 20, 2010

Last night on the bus, I was having a friendly conversation with the lady sitting next to me, and she said, "If you don't mind me saying, it looks like you have a touch of Bell's palsy."

The doctor's forceps injured me at birth, which paralyzed the muscles and nerves on the left side of my face. Although I had muscle- and nerve-transplant surgeries to correct it when I was a kid, I still have a crooked smile.

Apparently my forceps injury looks like Bell's palsy, because everyone who has ever had Bell's palsy or knows what Bell's palsy is thinks I have it and wants to comfort me by telling me Bell's palsy facts. When they find out it's not Bell's palsy they say, "That's too bad, because Bell's palsy goes away after a while."

It's rather strange to have complete strangers around the

world feel the need to point out flaws on your face. I have to keep explaining, "This is just what my face is like; it has been since birth. I don't have Bell's palsy."

Some people act really condescending and say things like, "Wow, you're doing really well for yourself. When I/my cousin/random person had Bell's palsy, I/they wouldn't leave the house."

For fuck's sake, people, I don't have Bell's palsy! Please don't act like I should be locked in a basement like Sloth from The Goonies.

It's not like telling someone they have something stuck in their teeth. Would you like to discuss your medical history with complete strangers in public places and with other strangers turning to look and stare?

The only area my forceps injury has really affected is my self-esteem, causing me to make some bad dating decisions. I was in a nine-year relationship with a guy I started dating when we were both fourteen years old. I stayed with him out of insecurity, thinking no one else would love me because of my crooked smile. He was a nice guy, but I was bored and curious to see what it would be like to be with someone else. The idea of getting married, buying a house, and producing children made me feel claustrophobic. In my early twenties, I would watch Oprah episodes about middle-aged, sexless marriages and cry because I felt like I was already in one. After our breakup, I was working at Health Nuts, where, at least once a week, one or more customers would ask me if I had Bell's palsy.

Six months later, I started dating the first guy who asked me out—Hank. Hank was an old friend from high school. In high school, Hank was really fat. After high school, Hank stopped eating and lost a bunch of weight quickly, causing all the skin on his torso to sag and hang like a deflated Ninja Turtle shell made of droopy flesh. We dated for a year until I took him to rehab when I was twenty-four years old. When he sobered up, he looked confused, like he had woken up in a random location and didn't know how he had gotten there. And then he dumped me. Hank had a secret addiction to painkillers, which explained why he also had a flaccid penis. After he dumped me, he moved back in with his family at a trailer park.

I should have noticed red flags with Hank (like the fact that he spent more quality time with his drug dealer Stank than with me), but I overlooked them because of my own insecurity. I never met Stank, but Hank told me that Stank was really fat, never showered, and smelled really bad, therefore, attaining the super sexy nickname Stank.

After Hank, guys seemed more interested in my boobs than my smile, and I attracted some real winners. Since I didn't know how to end my first nine-year relationship, I would only date guys I knew I could dump. I would choose guys who were unavailable on purpose. For me, it was like their abundant and blatantly obvious flaws were red flags, and I was the bull charging for them. I knew I had legitimate excuses to break up with them, so I dated them. In relationships, I made the conscious decision to sit in the emergency-exit seat so I could jump out whenever I got scared.

I went on one date with a cute surfer guy, Steve, who took me to his parents' house and introduced me to his parents before I realized it was a date. I thought he needed a designated driver because he drank a lot. He took me surfing at Stinson Beach during great white breeding season. Despite all of the shark-attack warning signs, I got in the water because I thought he was cute, and he promised to pull me out of the water before I was eaten if a shark bit me. I would have gotten back in the water with Steve, but he got back together with his ex-girlfriend.

Once while running at Spring Lake, I pretended to be lost to have an excuse to talk to a cute park ranger named Hal. I continued to run around Spring Lake a few times a week for months, trying to find Hal again. I never saw him again, but a guy sitting on a park bench asked me out to dinner. It was one week before I was going to get paid again, and I was hungry, and he seemed like he would pay for dinner. Being forced to make polite conversation with him at dinner seemed to be more appetizing than boxed macaroni and cheese waiting for me at home or raiding my mom's fridge for leftovers. I agreed to meet him at a Thai restaurant for dinner. I knew this wasn't a guy I was interested in dating. I just went for the free food. I politely listened to army-training stories. At dessert he told me he liked to rub mangoes on his face.

When I was twenty-five, I dated John, who had his fortieth birthday at a skate park. In addition to skateboarding, this forty-year-old only occasionally worked as a DJ, his mom paid his rent, he liked creating graffiti, and he had two kids by two different women. He took me to a funeral for pet rabbits, where he cried hysterically.

I thought John's friend Alan was gay because he wanted to become a woman. Alan told me the dick he planned to get removed was named Little Miss Donkey. I stopped spending time with Alan when he told me that he was in love with me and wanted to live in my ceiling.

Along with Alan, I attracted other guys I had absolutely no interest in, like my coworker Darrell. At Health Nuts, Darrell asked me out every few months, despite the fact that I began crying the first time he asked me out. When my shift would end, he would ask what I was doing after work and pretend to be fascinated with wherever I was going: "Really, the dentist? Who's your dentist?"

Once, I let Darrell donate blood with me. After that he would constantly ask when we could donate blood again. I would say, "Sorry, you can only donate blood every six to eight weeks."

Another Health Nuts coworker named Hardy invited me over to his house, where I watched him fold laundry. I was reassured by one of my other Health Nut coworkers that Hardy was in a twelve-step program, so at the very least I wouldn't have to take him to rehab. Hardy tried kissing me, or at least that's what I think he was trying to do. He unhinged his jaw and gagged me with his tongue. This was the only kiss I've had where I didn't feel lips. As I was trying not to choke on his tongue, he kicked the back of my knees, trying to knock me over onto his bed while simultaneously reaching up my shirt and yanking my breasts out of the bottom of my bra. I was less than impressed with Hardy's mating techniques. I managed to stay standing and walked out.

Also at Health Nuts was a young butcher named Jason who became obsessed with me. As he had a girlfriend already, I refused to go out with him. He told me I was a "hottie with a naughty body" and that if my ass had a Facebook page he would add himself as a fan. I found notes from him on my car windshield just about every day, and he sent me constant e-mails and text messages for over six months, pressuring me to go out with him. One day at work, he begged me to have breakfast with him. I screamed at him in the parking lot, "I don't want shady with a side of pancakes for breakfast."

A lot of the customers would hit on me at Health Nuts too. The floral department was in the corner of the store, where customers would trap me and tell me strange things. A man well into his fifties gave massages outside the store for pay. He cornered me saying, "You look like a doll. I like watching you work, and I would give you a massage for free." No thank you, sir.

I had only one date with Alejandro, whom I met at one of my art shows in San Francisco. He invited me to the De Young Museum in Golden Gate Park on a weekend afternoon. Alejandro had a boner at the museum and came up behind me, pressing it on my back, and grinding it up against me like a dog humping a leg while sucking on my neck. He gave me a hickey before we even had our first kiss. That's right, I was dry humped at a museum on a first date. The museum was really crowded. I just stood there in shock as a bunch of middle-aged women watched.

Then I dated Ricky. Ricky was really hot and liked to work out, which I thought was great at first because both my first two boyfriends had giant beer guts before they were twenty-five. Despite the fact that he was the most muscular, beautiful man I had ever seen in my entire life, I constantly had to reassure him that he wasn't fat. He only ate protein shakes, frozen broccoli, and canned chicken. The only day of the week he cheated on his diet was Sundays, so that is the only night we could go out on dinner dates. He went to the gym all the time to lift weights. Ricky told me, "I want my neck to be thicker than my head. I want to become a sheriff so that I can shoot bad guys and die a hero in a gunfight."

Ricky dumped me less than twenty-four hours after he told me he would be willing to die if he were allergic to me and after I had babysat his cat and grandma for four days straight. Believe it or not, it was Ricky who broke my heart so badly that I felt like a raw-skinned animal.

The last date I went on in California was with Kyle, a Health Nut customer. Kyle picked me up for our date in a kidnapper van: a giant, white, windowless van. I tried to ignore the fact that he was driving the same type of vehicle a kidnapper would use to lure small children into the back with promises of candy and a puppy. The date wasn't great for a variety of reasons. He told me he liked lying and that it was an adjustment for him to respect women. At the end of the night, Kyle said, "I lived in this van for three months."

I remained silent and didn't even look his way.

Kyle leaned over and spoke louder to make sure I heard this gem of a fact, "I lived in this van for three months!"

26

"Where did you shower?" was all I could think of to say.

"At the gym." Not missing a beat, he went on to say, "I'm thinking about moving back in. So I haven't felt this way in a long time. I'd really like to see you again."

"Are you seriously planning to move into your van?"

"You wouldn't be cool with that? I thought an artist would be cool with that. You can look in the back if you want. I put the board up to keep the light out while I slept," he said as he tapped on the board separating the seats from the back.

The kidnapper-van date was my rock bottom. I gave up. I am utterly confused how people date, much less get married and have children. I might have taken the book Eat, Pray, Love too literally like an instructions manual. Meditating didn't float my boat; I'm too restless and impatient. During my breakup with Hank, a friend took me to a Buddhist meeting, where we chanted "Nam Myoho Renge Kyo," and I felt at home on a cellular level. I consider myself an accidental Buddhist. Through chanting, I learned to love myself—flaws and all. The practice is about transformation, not perfection.

After chanting every morning and evening for a couple of years, I really understood the Buddhist philosophy that "true happiness comes from within," and I didn't see the point of dating at all. Dating is overrated. It's so much easier to be alone. I went to New Zealand, relieved by the fact that New Zealand's population has a hundred thousand fewer men than women. The universe had made it abundantly clear that my future husband, if he's out there, is not in California. He'll just have to find me in New Zealand. I'm my own knight in shining armor. I saved myself with Nam Myoho Renge Kyo.

SATURDAY, AUGUST 28, 2010

I moved out of the flooded flat. Now I'm renting a room in a three-bedroom house with two Kiwi guys, Liam and Blake, for housemates. The house is clean and cute and in Ponsonby. It's about a twenty-minute walk from the city center. Ponsonby is the trendy area in Auckland; Kiwis call it "flash" instead of "fancy." I'm probably not cool enough to live here. It looks like an A-frame dollhouse. The only problem with the house is that the staircase is really steep. I have already fallen down it and gotten a huge bruise on my butt.

I met Colin Mathura-Jeffree, who is a male model and one of the judges on the TV show New Zealand's Next Top Model. As expected, he is a beautiful man. He has dark hair, creamy caramel complexion, and piercing green-hazel eyes. He's friends with my flatmate Liam, and we went to see a movie together. I, of course, had no idea who he was. After the movie, he took me to a gelato shop and had me taste his banana, nuts, and chocolate gelato. After I tasted his gelato, he came back to our place and taught me how to walk down the steep stairs like a model, with my feet sideways so that I won't fall down again. He has really intense eyes and barely ever blinks.

TUESDAY, AUGUST 31, 2010

We've created a chore schedule to keep the house clean. While I was washing the dishes, my new flatmate Blake said, "I'm going to Hoover."

"What?"

"Hoover. I'm going to Hoover around the lounge," he explained.

"I have no idea what you're talking about."

I watched him closely, expecting him to start doing a dance of some kind.

"I'll just show you." He took out a vacuum and started vacuuming the living room.

SUNDAY, SEPTEMBER 5, 2010

There was a huge earthquake in a city called Christchurch in the South Island. Last night the house was shaking, and I told my flatmates I thought I felt the earthquake, but they said it was just the storm. The weather reports said that there are cold winds from Antarctica blowing through New Zealand. I guess it was just the Antarctic winds shaking the house last night.

WEDNESDAY, SEPTEMBER 8, 2010

Last night my flatmate Liam and I saw mice in our house. I

screamed and jumped from mice all night with my thirty-something, male, Kiwi flatmate.

Granola bars are called muesli bars here. I kept muesli bars, which the mice seemed to love, in my backpack. We saw one mouse in the house early in the night, and then right when I was falling asleep, I heard rustling and the crunching sounds of a mouse in my backpack right near my bed. I tried to move my backpack out of the room with a clothes hanger, but the mouse ran out. I screamed and woke up my flatmate. I ended up moving the backpack to the hallway and could hear it all night. I could hear it crawling around the room all night and dreamt one was on my pillow. I woke up screaming in the middle of the night and turned on the lights.

Liam's an actor and told me that he didn't know people could actually emit bloodcurdling screams like me. He said if he hears about any roles that involve screaming he'll let me know.

I barely slept and decided to take the Link bus instead of walking to work. On the Link bus, my contacts fell out of my eyes, and I lost them. Luckily I'm nearsighted and could see the computer screen at work, but everything else was blurry.

THURSDAY, SEPTEMBER 9, 2010

One of my coworkers in the basement had a Subway sandwich for lunch. I asked, "Do you really like Subway?"

"Oh, yes, it's very nice. They just opened up last year. Have you tried these?" He held up a bag of Doritos.

"Doritos? Yeah, why?"

"Doritos just got here two years ago. They're really nice!"

He visited America and tried Ben and Jerry's ice cream. I really wish they had that down here. I miss Phish Food ice cream.

SUNDAY, SEPTEMBER 12, 2010

Since I've been here, I've gotten a lot of weird questions about America and California. I feel like I need to do a Wikipedia search on my own country after having conversations with Kiwis. I haven't been to all fifty states, and I don't know anything about Native American burial rites or facts about Tennessee, the Appalachian Mountains, or Alaska. Even though I'm from California, I'm not friends with Paris Hilton and have never even met any celebrities.

California and New Zealand are around the same size. It's hard for me to wrap my head around how big America is and how small New Zealand is. I grew up in a small town called Petaluma in Sonoma County, about an hour north of San Francisco. Petaluma looks just like the suburbs you see on TV, but it's way more boring. I grew up in a cookie-cutter house in a cookie-cutter neighborhood, where all the streets were named after wines. The only thing Petaluma's famous for is being the place where the egg incubator was invented. At one point in time, Petaluma was the chicken capital of the world. For this reason, there's a Butter and Egg Day parade where small children are dressed up like baby chicks and walk in a parade down Petaluma Boulevard every year.

At Petaluma High School, there was a cow-plop contest every year as a fund-raiser. People would bet on a square in the courtyard of the high school, and someone would bring their cow in to school and walk the cow around the courtyard until it pooped on a square. Whoever's square the cow pooped on won the contest. Sonoma County is also known for smelling like cow plop. It's lovingly referred to as "Sonoma aroma."

There wasn't even a movie theater in town when I was growing up. Teens hung out in barns on Friday nights. At the age of fourteen, I had no other choice for entertainment but to have a homeless man named Snake buy me booze so that I could get drunk in public parks midday on the weekends.

MONDAY, SEPTEMBER 13, 2010

I've seen a cute guy who works on a different floor in the elevators. He never makes eye contact with me. I rode the elevator with him today. He asked which floor I was going to. That amount of human interaction with me made him visibly nervous. He fidgeted for all three floors I rode with him. His eyes darted around, he breathed heavily, and he seemed to be breaking out in a sweat. I could almost hear his heart racing. I just stood there staring at him out of the corner of my eye. When he got out of the elevator, he thanked me. I'm not sure what for. I'm not sure if that meant he liked me.

Something in between being stalked by guys in California and the silent treatment in New Zealand would be fantastic. I have never felt safer or more invisible.

At work there seem to be a lot of angry middle-aged women with Edward (from Twilight) posters and fireman calendars. These women give off the vibe that they haven't been touched by a man since the 1980s. When I walk by smiling, they look up at me glaring. They look me up and down, stare at my boobs, and never smile back.

I came to New Zealand to avoid dating, but I'm sincerely starting to fear I will never have sex again. I really don't want to become an angry middle-aged woman with Edward posters and fireman calendars in a cubicle.

I heard there's going to be a male brothel that services women opening. Prostitution is legal in New Zealand. I wonder what they'll charge.

TUESDAY, SEPTEMBER 14, 2010

It took me a while to get used to everything being on the left side here. It's not just the side of the street you drive on; walking down the sidewalk—or "footpath," as they call it—is also to the left, and escalators going up and down are reversed. I'm still looking the wrong way when I cross the street.

In grocery store aisles, I go down the right side, like in America, and accidentally ram my cart into everyone else. I found porridge, like in nursery rhymes, for sale at the grocery store. Do you have any idea how excited I was to see porridge in the grocery store? After ramming my cart into others at the grocery store, I ran home to taste what Goldilocks has been eating all these years. Porridge is oatmeal. It's a major letdown.

SUNDAY, SEPTEMBER 19, 2010

I found other Buddhists in Auckland, and we drove down to the opening ceremony of a peace park in Rotorua. During the opening ceremony, there were Maori chiefs blessing the grounds, speeches in Japanese, and local New Zealand Buddhists giving talks. It was amazing to see a diverse group of people completely respecting each other's differences.

Before driving back up to Auckland, we went in a natural hot-mud bath in our swimsuits—or "togs," as Kiwis call them. We got a bit lost in the dark on a country road somewhere between Rotorua and Auckland. There were hardly any street signs, just farmland and sheep. We stopped the car to look at a street sign, and all the sheep came up to the car and baaed at us.

I sat in the back seat with Cyan from New York. She's been living in New Zealand for seven years and is engaged to a comedian from New Zealand. She said I can go to his show with her sometime. Her accent sounds soft, sweet, and singsongy, like she should be a narrator for children's books.

WEDNESDAY, SEPTEMBER 22, 2010

I was watching TV with my flatmate Blake. There are only four channels on New Zealand TV. As we watched TV, Blake said, "I bet America has so many channels on TV," he paused, trying to think of a large number, "like forty!"

I laughed so hard I could hardly breathe.

He sounded astonished, "You have more than forty channels in America?"

"Yeah, we have a lot of channels."

A program I thought was a parody show, like John Stewart's The Daily Show, came on. They announcer said, "There has been a record-breaking number of police officers shot in the past two years. Two police officers have been shot in the past two years. This is outrageous! Australia hasn't had a police officer shot in eight years!"

I laughed at what I thought was a comedian and asked, "What are we watching?"

"The news."

"Are you joking? Two cops in two years! Are you serious? That's a slow day in Oakland."

FRIDAY, SEPTEMBER 24, 2010

The German girl I met at the hostel took me to a play called the Masculine Monologues. It was held at a café called the Te Karanga Gallery on K' Road. K' Road is short for Karangahape Road. It's really close to the city center but is known for being the red-light district, where all the prostitutes are. I hear the director Thomas Sainsbury is the most prolific playwright and director in New Zealand. It looks like he's also the most popular—I was lucky to get a seat. It was so crowded some people were standing.

I wasn't really sure what to expect; I thought maybe it would be guys talking about their penises, like the male version of the Vagina Monologues, but it was a series of monologues about being a man. My favorite was the last one, performed by Roberto Nascimento. He seemed as vulnerable as he was funny.

TUESDAY, SEPTEMBER 28, 2010

Today at work, the entire team huddled around me and looked at my white American teeth. They laughed at how white and straight my teeth were. I didn't realize I had good teeth before I left America. In America, I had to get braces for an under bite and gaps between my teeth. I've had dozens of cavities filled since my childhood. When I was a kid, I had so many cavities that I stopped opening my mouth for my dentist and had to go to a specialty dentist for children.

My dad is obsessed with flossing. He flosses constantly. He even flosses in the car while driving. He hates the feeling of having anything stuck between his teeth.

As an adult, my anal-retentive dental hygienist would nag me about flossing. She would scoff when I told her I only changed my toothbrush every few months. My gums would bleed, and my jaw would ache as they scraped plaque, making that horrible noise. As she scraped my teeth, she would mock my dentist for having so many clothes for her pet Chihuahuas. They had their own clothes closet in her house.

The hygienist tried to get me to buy electric toothbrushes and teeth bleach. She told me I had bad genes that made my gums bad. Flossing once a day wasn't enough. I was instructed to brush and floss every time I ate anything and to change my toothbrush once a month.

American advertising and my dentist convinced me I had stained teeth that needed whitening. I bought cheap over-the-counter whitening strips that turned my gums red and raw and made my teeth overly sensitive for weeks after. I was aware that anything that could stain a carpet could stain your teeth, and I would wipe my teeth off with a napkin after drinking coffee if I was unable to brush. Self-conscious, I would examine my teeth in mirrors after all meals.

Today, they all pointed and laughed, "Your teeth are so American looking!"

MONDAY, OCTOBER 4, 2010

Over the weekend, we decided to throw a flat-warming party. Saturday before the party, Liam, Blake, and I went shopping for decorations for the party.

I wandered outside, where I saw a hot guy promoting the Paralympics. It's been my observation that straight guys like sports. Evolution got this one wrong. Gay guys should have evolved to be interested in sports so that I don't have to pretend to be interested in sports when I have a boyfriend or if I want to make conversation with a straight guy.

The Paralympics promoter was sitting behind a table filled with pictures of the athletic limbless. He had a boyish charm, sparkling green eyes, and a devilish grin. I stood in front of the table, stared into his eyes, and smiled back at him.

"Hi, do you know about the Paralympics?"

"No, but I would like to know more," I lied.

He went on and on about the Paralympics. I kept staring and nodding my head, pretending to listen but not listening to a word he was saying. He asked me, "Are you from the States? Do you watch basketball? I love basketball!"

"Yes, we have basketball, but I don't watch any sports. I do yoga, but I don't think that could be considered a competitive sport."

As I'm trying to chat this guy up, my flatmates come out of the store and say, "There you are, Jamie, we've been looking all over the store for you." They looked impatient and anxious to get home to decorate. The hot Paralympics promoter's eyes were bouncing between us, trying to figure out if I was in a relationship.

"These are my flatmates!" I said too quickly. I defensively explained, "We're throwing a party and shopping for it." I looked back at my flatmates, who know I'm not remotely interested in any sports whatsoever and told them, "I'll meet you back in the car."

When I went back to the car, I showed my flatmates the pin the hot Paralympics promoter sold me for twenty dollars. They convinced me to invite him to the party. I wrote my name, address, and phone number on a piece of paper. My heart was racing. When I get nervous, my clumsiness is amplified. I got out of the car and hit my shin on the car parked next to us. Not wanting to limp up to the Paralympics promoter, I composed myself and then walked back to his table.

"You're back?"

"Here's the info for the party tonight, if you happen to be free." I threw the piece of paper at him and ran away quickly, before I could be rejected.

I heard him say, "You live in Ponsonby?" I didn't respond as I sprinted back to the car.

When I got back to the car, my flatmates asked me

something I had not considered up until this point: "Does he have legs?"

"I don't know, he was sitting behind a table, I couldn't see. Whatever, I like being on top anyway. He's so hot, it doesn't matter as long as his third leg works. Do you think you can climb stairs with prosthetic legs?"

The angle of the stairs at our house is ladderlike. The steps are so narrow that I have to tiptoe up and down with my small feet. I've fallen down the stairs twice now. If this guy didn't have legs, it was going to be difficult to get him up the stairs to my bedroom. Panicked, I was having visions of one of my flatmates carrying my legless lad up the steep stairs and laying him on my bed for me to have my way with him. I prayed he had three fully intact and functioning legs.

A few hours later, I received a text message, "Hey is this Jamie? This is Freddy, the happy sales guy from today. Would love to come tonight but headed out of town. Maybe another night?"

Trying to sound casual, I texted back, "Hey Freddy, this is Jamie. Another night sounds good. Safe travels."

At the party, I got drunk and told some of my flatmate's lesbian friends about Freddy, the hot Paralympics promoter. I told them, "I'm not sure if he has legs, but I don't care."

They found the story funny, and one of them told me, "Once I was getting out of my car with my girlfriend at the time, and there were three guys in wheelchairs. One of them rolled up to me and said, 'Are you a lesbian?' I said back to him, 'Are you a cripple?'"

The next morning, I woke up still drunk and starving. I was too drunk to walk up the street to get food, and we had no food in the house. It was ten in the morning, and I called KFC, begging them to please deliver me food, but they said no. I went online to try to find somewhere nearby that would deliver on a Sunday at ten and noticed I had a message on my Facebook wall from one of my new lesbian friends: "Hey mate! How about yoga this Friday?"

In my drunkenness the night before, I had told my new friend that, in addition to being sexually frustrated, I enjoyed yoga. I cringed as I recalled telling them, "I haven't had a boyfriend in over a year. I asked out someone without legs so that he couldn't run away from me."

I still haven't heard from Freddy, the possible paraplegic. I sent him a text that said, "It was nice to meet you, maybe when you are back in town we can go on a hike or to the beach? Good luck with the donations."

I never heard back. My flatmates reckon he had no legs and was too embarrassed to tell me he can't walk in sand with his fake legs.

TUESDAY, OCTOBER 5, 2010

Next to Ponsonby is Herne Bay, where I like running.

There are little beaches down most of the streets. After my runs, I go down to the beach at the end of Hamilton Road and stretch. Hamilton Beach has pohutukawa trees with branches that lie lazily over the sand. The tree branches are the perfect height to prop my foot up on to stretch my legs after a long run. I also like lying in the branches of the trees to stretch my back and arms. It's bliss to lie in the branches and look up at the clouds and hear the waves.

Today after a long run, I was stretching in my tree as usual. All winter I had the beach to myself, but now that it was turning into spring and the sun was shining, there were other people at my beach. I didn't pay attention to the other people; I was in my own world, sweaty, stretching, and enjoying nature.

Out of nowhere, a middle-aged man approached me, "Can I show you how to do that stretch correctly? I'm a yoga instructor." He propped his leg up on the tree next to me and started lecturing me about yoga.

This is the type of thing that would happen in California, but it hadn't happened to me in New Zealand up until this point. I had let my guard down since being here. Most guys don't even make eye contact with me. Dating and procreation in this country are a mystery to me.

In California, I was used to being harassed by most males I crossed paths with. This was the first noticeable difference about New Zealand. When walking the streets, no one turns their heads at my curves, as if crossing the international date line put me in a burka.

Everyone is so proper in New Zealand, even the construction workers don't whistle at you. For me, it was normal to tell guys who were whistling, shouting vulgar things, honking horns, following me, or trying to get me to get in their cars to "fuck off" while flipping them off in the streets of California. I grew numb to it; it was just a fact that I needed to carry pepper spray and pretend I didn't speak English if I wanted to remain untouched by strangers.

There I was, standing on a quiet beach in New Zealand, dazed from the endorphin release from my run. I was unguarded, trying to remember what it is I do and say to get out of situations like this, such as stretching lessons from creepy old guys who sneak up on you.

Wearing faded jeans and an old gray sweatshirt that matched his hair, he continued with his leg propped up on the tree branch and while snickering told me, "This stretch is good for opening your pelvis."

I cringed; I could feel myself glaring at him as I backed away to remain out of his reach. He was picking up on my vibes that I was less than impressed with his unsolicited yoga lessons, and he tried to make it better by telling me how to open my pelvis by saying, "I'm really a yoga instructor. I give lessons at a nearby studio. You should come by for a lesson."

"No thanks."

"Running, it irritates your heart."

"Well my dad's nearly sixty, and he's a marathon runner and runs in the Boston marathon all of the time, and he looks really good for his age. He looks way younger than you."

Maybe if I point out to the yoga instructor that he's hitting on a girl young enough to be his daughter the pelvis-opening lessons will end.

"I saw you stretching with your back on the tree branch; you have a nice open chest. I'm not being dodgy," he explained, snickering and starring at my natural Ds.

My eyebrows rise. The more someone has to tell you they aren't dodgy, the dodgier they really are. Every nerve and fiber in my being was grossed out. The only stretches he was interested in showing me are opening my pelvis and chest. No thank you, sir. I had a queasy feeling and the urge to run. I don't want him to follow me home, so the only defense I can think of is to continue to talk about my dad. He finally got the hint that I thought he was a creep and left.

WEDNESDAY, OCTOBER 6, 2010

There's a little old man who volunteers in the basement where I work. At morning tea, he asked me, "Have you met any nice blokes?"

"Not any straight ones."

He choked on his tea, and we sat in silence for the rest of

morning tea.

TUESDAY, OCTOBER 12, 2010

Attempting to network and make friends, I went to an American Women's Club meeting. I sat at a round table with about a dozen undersexed, bored, middle-aged housewives.

We all introduced ourselves. Most were relocated to New Zealand because of their husbands and missed the great US of A.

The women were excited to see a youthful face at the table. Most of them had daughters my age. One asked, "Are you single?"

I nodded and blushed.

"I have a single daughter in her late twenties in the States, and I want grandchildren. What's the dating scene like? How are Kiwi guys?"

"I have no idea," I shrugged. "They are more elusive than the endangered kiwi bird. I hadn't even made eye contact with a straight one. I've just had my second very cold winter this year. With the uneven ratio of one hundred thousand more women than men, if you have a daughter with a ticking biological clock, don't bring her to New Zealand."

One woman worked at the men's prison as a librarian. She said, "My favorite time of day is watching the prisoners

45

come out of the showers." She nodded and added, "Uh-huh, oh yeah," fanning her face.

All the sexually-starved women at the table squirmed and groaned with envy. I'm beginning to panic; I may not have sex ever again if I stay in New Zealand.

THURSDAY, OCTOBER 14, 2010

I watched Hotel, six short plays by Thomas Sainsbury. His writing is so funny. The Te Karanga Gallery is a great space, but it just can't hold all the people wanting to watch the shows. He's going to have to find a larger venue.

FRIDAY, OCTOBER 15, 2010

I've heard travel horror stories about people's misadventures on tour buses in New Zealand. There are a variety of buses to choose from, and it's the cheapest way to see the country, but I think it's the type of thing where you get what you pay for.

Every person I have talked to has told me the buses are filled with really annoying people who get really drunk and have sex in their hostel room with others in the room. I know more than one person who has been on the bottom bunk with people having sex on the top bunk.

One girl who recently went to the South Island was in a six-sleeper room, where everyone was having one-night stands expect for her and a Scottish guy. One of the guys

46

passed out mid-thrust. As his date scampered off, the Scottish guy who wasn't having sex took a razor and dry-shaved the passed out guy's naked, drunk body, even his eyebrows.

I don't know if I was ever young enough or if I could ever be drunk enough to enjoy this type of touring.

SATURDAY, OCTOBER 16, 2010

I've been training to run a 10K in the Auckland Marathon. Blake, my flatmate, sometimes runs with me. I went to see a Kids of 88 and Naked and Famous concert with my friend Natalie (from the basement) and Blake. Natalie and I drank whiskey and ginger beer and danced together.

After the concert, I had the idea to run to the beach with Blake. Drunk, I took off sprinting—the beach is just a few blocks away. I ran across a street without looking and ran in front of a cop car. Not expecting a drunk run, Blake was having trouble keeping up with me. To the cop I ran in front of, it probably looked like he was chasing me, and the cop started following us. I hid behind a bush in the front yard of a fancy-looking house near the beach. I whispered to Blake, "I don't want to get deported for being drunk."

Not a lot happens in New Zealand. When I first got here, "Wild Goose Attacks Child" accompanied by a photo of a squawking goose was on the front page of the newspaper. There's a New Zealand version of the American TV show Cops. In America on Cops, cops with guns chase toothless

47

crackheads with guns. On the New Zealand version, cops politely drive drunk people home and tell them how to cure hangovers.

TUESDAY, OCTOBER 19, 2010

Cyan, the sweet girl from New York, invited me to a filming of her fiancé Steve's TV show, 7 Days. The studio is just down the street from my house on Ponsonby Road. It was fun to be in the audience and watch what goes on behind the scenes. Steve's really funny and down to earth. Cyan and Steve are so cute together. You can just tell they really love and respect each other.

THURSDAY, OCTOBER 21, 2010

Colin Mathura-Jeffree kindly gave my flatmate Liam four tickets to go to a movie premier. Liam invited me, our other flatmate Blake, and Thomas Sainsbury. I've never been to anything like that before. It was all very exciting; there were cocktail waitresses with fancy drinks on platters walking around and a buffet of free food. Blake and I were a bit out of our element and in awe of it all.

Blake said what sounded like, "Oh my God, I can't believe Juan Nooze is here!"

"Who's he? Is he a celebrity?" I scanned the crowded room of flash-looking people for a Latino male celebrity figure.

"No, Juan Nooze."

"What does he look like?"

"No, Juan Nooze!" Blake turned and pointed to a TV cameraman filming the event. The side of his camera had the One News logo on it.

"Oh, One News!"

WEDNESDAY, OCTOBER 27, 2010

I watched a play called Idiots: Back 2 School. It had the girl from Whale Rider in it. She's grown up now and absolutely beautiful.

THURSDAY, OCTOBER 28, 2010

On Monday, I was assigned a new task doing data entry that I finished within a couple of hours. I've just been writing stories about dating in California since then. Since I've been typing, everyone has assumed I've been doing data entry. This afternoon I ran out of stories to write and thought I should do some actual work. I asked my boss for my next task. It was around half past three. He looked at the clock and said, "Have a Kit Kat."

"What?"

"Take a break. Have a Kit Kat."

FRIDAY, OCTOBER 29, 2010

I was invited to happy-hour birthday drinks for a girl who I find a bit overwhelming, or "full on," as Kiwis say. I've been working in the basement doing data entry for five months. I've very limited social interaction underground.

Over a year ago, before I left for New Zealand, I began boycotting dating. I would spend most of my Friday and Saturday nights with my mom or grandma. My mother was beginning to think her then-twenty-six-year-old daughter would never produce grandchildren because I had chosen Friday night to be my laundry night. My mother even told me, "You might not find someone until you're in your fifties because you act like a middle-aged person."

But at this point, at happy hour in November, my mom and grandma stopped asking me if I had been on any dates because the answer was always no. At five o'clock, I emerged from the silent basement, where my boss said, "Are you feeling OK? You look very pale."

"That's because I am. I'm feeling fine, it's just that I'm Irish, Scottish, Norwegian, German, and English. My ancestors didn't get much sun, and I've had two back-to-back winters, and I've been in a basement for five months."

I tried to not act like my awkward, pale self and forced a smile when I reached the table of twenty- and thirty-somethings at the bar. I waved hello to everyone. The birthday girl overwhelmed me with a hug, pulled a chair from another table, placed it in between two guys, and told

50

me to sit down. I sat down, hoping I was not getting set up with either of the short, plain-looking guys I was sitting between.

The birthday girl sat across the table from me; there were two other girls on either side of her. Including me, there was a total of six people at the table, four of whom I had not seen before. Before introductions, the birthday girl blurts out across the table at me, "Jamie, guess what? I moved in with two really hot guys. They're always down for a hookup; you should totally come over and meet them. You would really like them."

All heads at the table turned toward me. I could feel my face burning. What did the other people at the table think of me now?

"Umm, no thank you." Was she their pimp? Was she living at a male brothel? "That sounds like the complete opposite of what I would be interested in."

I think my lack of sex life is becoming palpable. My need to be touched feels like a throbbing, raw, exposed nerve. I heard that orphaned babies die if they are not held, even if they receive the proper nutrition.

The conversation didn't end there; everyone began talking sex at me. I was a deer stuck in sex lights, unsure how I became the center of this conversation or how to get out of it. I didn't know what to say to these strangers, so I said, "I don't know how dating works in this country. No one makes eye contact with me. Once I was riding the elevator at work, and a guy who works in a different part of the building made eye contact with me." That was the only thing I could contribute to this New Zealand casual-sex conversation—making eye contact in an elevator.

The short graying guy to my left (who I later found out is a boy scout and goes on weekend scout retreats) turned toward me and said, "People don't really date in this country. Everyone just has one-night stands. There's no motivation to date if you can just get sex whenever you want it."

"Well, I guess I'm never having sex in New Zealand."

Perhaps, this wasn't birthday drinks—maybe I was in some kind of intervention? Instead of trying to force me to rehab, they were trying to convince me to get out more and get laid.

SUNDAY, OCTOBER 31, 2010

I ran a 10K in the Auckland Marathon today. I overslept and was a bit hung over from going to a Halloween party with Liam and his friends Lulu and Colin Mathura-Jeffree last night. I wasn't planning to go out, with the race the next day, but Colin and the rest of Liam's friends came over all dressed up and looking glamorous. Liam was dressed as a sexy vampire. Liam and his friends are all ridiculously good looking. They all are models or should be models, not just Colin. Liam has a friend named Lulu who looks like a Barbie doll come to life, but more beautiful and muscular. She used to be a professional

52

female wrestler. Lulu is tall, tan, blonde, blue eyed, full lipped, and toned. She looks fake, but she hasn't had any work done; she's naturally better looking than Barbie.

Once I went to the beach with Liam and Lulu, the dynamic duo. Lulu radiated like a golden goddess as she sunbathed. I remained fully dressed and hid under a large hat next to her like squishy, pale dough.

Last night Colin said, "You're coming with us, hurry, get dressed."

"I don't have a costume."

"You could dress as Bella from Twilight; do you have any emo-girl clothes?" Colin asked.

"That's all I have."

Last night was fun, but this morning I sprinted from my house in Ponsonby and down to Victoria Park where the race began. All the runners had already left; I started running with the slow walkers. Eventually, I caught up to the other runners and finished the 10K. I walked back home after, passing by the flash cafés with outdoor seating that I can't afford to eat at. I was bright red and sweaty and still had my race number pinned to my chest. Some rich-looking people sipping cappuccinos outside looked grossed out by me when I walked by all sweaty. They asked me, "Are you lost? The race is in town."

"Yeah, I know, I just ran it. I'm walking home now."

TUESDAY, NOVEMBER 2, 2010

I can't tell the difference between American and Canadian accents. There are, of course, some obvious differences between, let's say, a French-Canadian accent and a New York or Southern accent, but for the most part, the standard American accent you hear in movies and TV sounds nearly identical to the standard Canadian accent—at least to my ignorant Californian ears. The only way I can tell if someone is Canadian is if they sound American but say "eh" at the end of their sentences.

On the bus, I heard what sounded like an American family talking behind me. I found it comforting to hear a familiar accent. Excited to make friends with other internationally traveling Americans, I turned around and said with a smile, "What state are you from?"

They glared at me, "We're Canadian!"

"Oh, sorry, I thought you were American."

To me, hearing the difference between American and Canadian accents is more difficult than tasting the perceived range of complex sensory descriptors wine connoisseurs claim to taste. After swirling, sniffing, and sipping, I can taste red or white and good or bad, not earthy, chocolate, raspberry, oak, pepper, citrus fruit, smoke, honey, or gooseberry. Sorry, Canadians, but you sound like me.

WEDNESDAY, NOVEMBER 3, 2010

Just like "biscuits," the word "rooting" has a completely different meaning in New Zealand than it does in California. In California, one would say they need to get rooted when they settle in somewhere, as in, to put down roots, to ground themselves. After living oblivious to the New Zealand definition for five months and while brushing my teeth with Liam the other night, I told him, "I'm really excited to live in this house because I really need to get rooted. I traveled all around Samoa for a month before I came here, and the first place I lived in New Zealand didn't work out, so I had to move. I'm excited to stay in one place long enough to get rooted."

Liam's eyes almost popped out of his head, and he just about choked on his toothbrush. He spat out his toothpaste, staring at me out of the corner of his eye. Finally he spoke, "Jamie, are you hitting on me? Do you know what rooting means here?"

"No, I'm not hitting on you. Of course I know what rooting means. It means to get grounded, settle in, to put down roots. I need to get rooted; I'm tired of traveling."

Smiling he explained, "Rooting has a different definition in New Zealand than in the States; it means to have sex, but more rude. It's like saying, 'I need to get fucked.'"

My jaw dropped, I turned bright red. I was mortified. I had been in the country for months—how many other people had I told I needed to get rooted? When I was asked in job interviews how long I was planning to stay in Auckland, did I say, "I was planning to be here for a while because I really need to get rooted?"

THURSDAY, NOVEMBER 4, 2010

My contract for data entry in the basement is almost up. I had another job interview with a different temp agency at half past seven this morning.

My interviewer was late. A woman rushed through the doors at quarter of eight and went up to the receptionist, "Is she here yet?"

"Yes."

"OK," my interviewer panted and then ran off, presumably to get coffee in the office kitchen. After a few moments, she emerged, looking like she had been out partying and had just rolled out of bed wearing the clothes she passed out in.

"Good morning, I'll be interviewing you in here," she said while pointing to a room. I followed her in. As we sat, she apologized, "Sorry I'm late. I live alone, but I'm not lonely. If I get lonely, I go to my neighbor's."

Not sure of how to respond, I nodded and remained quiet. After a few get-to-know-you, why-are-you-in-the-country, how-long-are-you-staying questions, she looked me up and down. "Where did you get that dress? It's a designer dress huh? Is it from the States?"

"One of my friends cleaned out her closet and gave it to me. I didn't know the designer's name." I sat cross-legged in black, knee-high boots and an olive, curve-hugging, retro-inspired Veronika Maine dress. I worried my outfit might have been too sexy for my interview to be a receptionist working with recently released prisoners. I'm all curves—ordinary clothes become scandalous when they caress my body.

She continued to rave about my dress, complaining about the shopping in New Zealand. She began calling me "James" and "Love" as if we were old friends catching up over coffee. I tried to rein the interview in. I asked, "Where is the prison?"

"Oh, it's not at the prison, it's near the prison, over there," she said while pointing out the window, as if that narrowed it down for me.

I told her, "I'm actually not familiar with the area the prison is in. Is the prison on the Link bus route? What's the street and name of the company?"

"I don't know the street. I think this is the name of the company," she scribbled down a name in loopy letters and put an exclamation mark at the end. She might as well have written, "Yay for prisoners!" Then she explained in a serious tone, "Confidentiality is very important in this job; you may see the recently released prisoners at a bar or something on your time off."

Then she grimaced and looked down as if this happened to her and said, "I know I could be pashing someone on the weekend, and they could be my client Monday morning."

Pashing means kissing in New Zealand. At this point, I was becoming very aware I had not drank nearly as much coffee as I needed to think of appropriate responses for this interview. All I could think to say was, "This is a small country. I am aware I'm on an island and need to be conscious of my actions."

I think her bad-boy complex was worse than mine, because she said, "These guys really deserve a second chance, and they're trying to turn their lives around. I know guys back home that would get in fights at the pub and punch another guy in the head, then that guy's head would hit the brick wall behind them, and then they would be dead, and then the guy would go away with manslaughter, which is really unfair."

I smiled politely, "I'm sure it wasn't their intention to kill them."

She continued to ramble endlessly about all things not pertaining to the job, and I continued to pry information out of her by asking things like, "When does the job start and how much does it pay?"

FRIDAY, NOVEMBER 12, 2010

I promised not to pash the prisoners, and Monday morning I started as a receptionist working with ex-convicts who were a little too excited to meet me. They hadn't seen a woman in years until they saw me, but they were still more polite than guys in California. They had the male equivalent to female stripper's names. My favorite was Storm. The ex-cons would say, "What's your name? Where are you from? How long are you working here for?"

Unless you've given birth to one of the X-Men, don't name your kid Storm. He'll either end up a stripper or in jail.

I lasted one week. I was fired for making the same mistakes as the temp before me. They didn't bother telling me what the mistakes were, and I didn't care enough to ask. At half past three, they told me it was my last day.

At half past four, they told me to turn off the computer and stop answering the phones and then offered me beer. I politely complied and decided to drink as much free beer as I could. As I chugged beer on the clock, they explained further, "The last two people the temp agency sent weren't up to par."

I'm sure the mysterious coincidences I had with the temp before me had nothing to do with the training or the amount of beer in the building. The fridges at the office were completely filled with beer—every shelf. I was told the beers were for meetings; they weren't alcoholics. All of the garbage cans I emptied during my one week reeked of beer.

Between chugs of beer, I smiled and said, "That's fine. Look, I majored in art; I'm really not interested in this."

At five I said my final good-bye and stumbled out the door with a big smile on my face, knowing I would never be back.

SATURDAY, NOVEMBER 13, 2010

You know you've been living with guys for too long when you don't think twice about washing your hands with powder laundry detergent.

WEDNESDAY, NOVEMBER 17, 2010

I began my third job in New Zealand—shredding administrator. Despite the job title, the job does not involve shredding.

I worked in a room with eight other twenty-something international temps. There were Tyler, Adam, and Alice from England; Daniel and Aileen from Ireland; a guy named Connor and a girl named Jody from New Zealand; David from Mexico; and American me.

There was a gray-haired woman wearing expensive designer clothes named Geraldine who showed me to the room and team I would work with. Technically Geraldine was our boss but only came into the office to check on us at half past four in the afternoon on Monday through Thursday; she had Fridays off. No one really knows what Geraldine does the rest of the day.

Our office is located in a government building in the city

center. Despite the professional setting, the job is like having a substitute teacher in grade school, except even the substitute teacher wasn't there.

On my first day, English Tyler trained me in how to be a shredding administrator. The room was filled with recall boxes filled with city development files. Tyler had a bad-boy charm: he had stubble from not shaving, messy golden hair that he didn't bother brushing, a mischievous grin, and blue eyes that looked every girl up and down. He was extremely hung over while training me. It was a Tuesday.

The job entailed taking a file out of a box, opening the file, removing staples from documents, looking at the document inside, and placing a gold-colored document separator sheet between each document. The document-separator sheet had a list of possible documents, including application, certificate, checklist, report, letter, plan, or other.

Tyler gave me expert advice, such as, "You see how this piece of paper has a 'to' and 'from' with a signature? That is a letter. Tick the box 'letter' on the gold sheet, put it in front of the letter, and turn the page. See how this piece of paper says 'application for blah, blah, blah?' Tick the box 'application.' If you take longer than thirty seconds to decide what type of document it is, just tick 'other.' There will be a lot of others."

We went through our first file together, separating each document with a gold sheet until the file doubled in size. Once finished I asked, "Do we shred it now? Where are the shredders?"

Tyler laughed, "No, there's another team that does the shredding. Just put the file back in the box when you're done."

"That's it?"

"Yes, but make sure your ticks stay in the lines. The shredding team gets upset if your ticks go outside the lines. And watch out for photocopied staples—they get me every time."

I had to bite my lip to prevent from laughing during my training. How was this government running if they were paying us to simply tick the correct box? Some of them sing along to music playing on the radio, some dance, and everyone tells jokes and laughs. The guys have push-up contests and make forts out of the boxes. There's a tennis ball and umbrella that we use to play cricket; we just have to try not to hit the ball against the walls of neighboring offices.

THURSDAY, NOVEMBER 18, 2010

Daniel, the Irish guy, came into work with the palms of his hands raw and blistered. He said he slipped while doing pull-ups at the gym. A few moments after he explained why his hands were raw and blistered, he talked about the movie he and Tyler went to the night before.

"Is that the real reason your hands are blistered?" I asked

with a giggle.

Given the unprincipled work environment, I thought that implying Daniel's hands were raw from giving Tyler a hand job would make everyone laugh. Wrong. All eyes were on the new American girl with a dirty mind. No laughs or smiles. A few jaws dropped. Everyone got the joke—they knew what I implied—but found no humor in it. The Irish girl Aileen finally broke the silence and stares by saying, "That came out of nowhere."

Within a few minutes, Tyler began complaining about the job, and Daniel said, "You're so hard to please."

FRIDAY, NOVEMBER 19, 2010

I'm really excited to not be in a basement or working with ex-cons and to be working with other traveling twenty-somethings, but they don't seem excited to get to know me. I was so excited to see a Mexican because I'm from California; I miss hearing Spanish. I was like, "Hola, amigo, I'm your neighbor, I'm from California!"

He just said, "Hey," and looked away.

They were all practicing each other's accents. I told them, "Your accents sound lyrical to me, and how does my accent sound to you?"

Tyler replied, "You sound like a fucking Yank."

After they found out I didn't know about Commonwealth sports, Daniel said, "That's because you don't care about anything outside your own country."

I'm actually oblivious to sports in general, including American sports. I'm a little artist; how am I supposed to know the rules of cricket?

As much as they act like they hate me and America, all they talk about are American TV shows and American pop stars. I made them chocolate-chip cookies to try to get them to warm up to me. They ate the cookies but were not impressed when I told them how it was funny that they call cookies biscuits and that we have something else in America similar to a scone that we call a biscuit.

I told them, "I was really missing American biscuits so I got my grandma's biscuit recipe and went grocery shopping with my flatmates. I asked my flatmates, do you have Crisco in this country? It's a vegetable shortening used to make biscuits.

"My flatmate, the one that told me the New Zealand definition of rooting, just started laughing at me. He told me, 'I only know what Crisco is from living in the States. Gay guys use it there for fisting. The only place you are going to find Crisco in New Zealand is at a sex shop on K road.'

"I just told him, 'Oh. Well, my grandma's biscuit recipe calls for Crisco, that's why I asked.'

"My other flatmate was homeschooled and really innocent.

He honestly thought gynecologists worked with dinosaurs. He almost jumped out of the moving car when he heard about Crisco fisting."

None of them laughed at that story or even made eye contact with me.

SATURDAY, NOVEMBER 20, 2010

My grandma was angry with me when I decided to come here. She said, "No, don't go to New Zealand, you're going to get married and never come back." After being here for months, she asked me, "Have you met any nice boys; have you been on any dates?"

The answer was always no. No guys look at me or talk to me. I have no idea how dating works in this country. I told my grandma, "I don't think anyone wants to date me since I'm American. America is universally hated. I have been made fun of for being American by people from New Zealand, England, Ireland, and India."

My grandma's response was, "Well, we bailed out most of those countries during the war, and we buy things from all of those countries and stimulate their economy. They should be nicer to you."

When my grandma says, "the war," she is talking about World War II. Somehow I don't think telling a hot guy who hates me for being American that, "According to my grandma, we bailed you out in World War II, and she says you should be nicer to me. Also, America stimulates the world economy by being mass consumers, how about you stimulate me?" is going to help me find love.

MONDAY, NOVEMBER 22, 2010

My coworkers were talking about what they did over the weekend, and one said they watched the TV show 7 Days because they think Steve Wrigley's funny. I thought this would be a conversation they would let me join. I said, "Steve's really nice and funny. One of my friends is engaged to him."

"How do you know him?"

"I practice Buddhism, and his fiancée is Buddhist, that's how I met her. She's from America too, from a little town in New York State. She's seriously the nicest person I've ever met. Sometimes I go to his shows with her or watch 7 Days getting filmed."

"You're not a Buddhist."

"I am, actually."

"No, you're not."

"I chant 'Nam Myoho Renge Kyo.'" After an awkward silence, I tried to explain further, "There are actually millions of people practicing in over 192 countries all over the world. There's a lot of Buddhists in Auckland and a center not too far out of town."

Trying to break the silence, "Do you like New Zealand's

66

Next Top Model? Do you know Colin Mathura-Jeffree? He's really nice too."

TUESDAY, NOVEMBER 23, 2010

We took the elevator to go one floor down during a tea break.

There was awkward silence in the elevator, and Tyler said, "What would you do if you were trapped in the lift and you had to take a shit?"

Tyler had thought about it and had a plan; he said, "I'd shit in my shoe."

WEDNESDAY, NOVEMBER 24, 2010

Everyone at this job is traveling in New Zealand with a friend or partner. When they found out I came to New Zealand alone, they looked at me like I have the plague. One young English guy traveling with his girlfriend told me, "It really is a much nicer experience to share with someone else."

I haven't had the typical backpacker's experience of New Zealand. I've hardly made it out of Auckland. I haven't been to the South Island or to many happy hours. New Zealand is about grounding, centering, and healing myself. I'm almost too content to stay in, writing, painting, and reading all day.

67

They all went on and on about how much better it is to travel with someone you're in love with or friends with.

I said, "Don't you think I would have traveled with someone if I had the option?"

Thanks for rubbing in my loneliness.

THURSDAY, NOVEMBER 25, 2010

One of my coworkers said, "I heard, with the recession, that shaken-baby-syndrome incidents have risen."

Jokingly, I said, "I hear that studies show shaking a baby is a great form of stress relief."

No one laughed at that joke.

A few minutes later, we heard a baby crying in the room next door, and I said, "Told you so."

FRIDAY, NOVEMBER 26, 2010

Below are real e-mails from my boss Geraldine to the shredding team in response to us playing cricket on the clock:

-----Original Message-----

Ciao,

I have received an e-mail about the noise coming from the Kiwi Room. I understand you have been asked by the business to stop the noise but have continued. I do not know who is responsible for the balls bouncing off walls and the cheering, but you will know. You are in a work environment. When you need relaxation, you can go outside during your breaks.

I have worked in project teams, often in a separate room or an area away from the main business teams, so I do understand that sometimes you feel isolated enough not to feel part of the business and so act in a way that assumes no one else is disrupted. However, once you have been told that your noise is disruptive to another team, you need to stop it.

I am disappointed that this has happened, as you are hardworking individuals and a good team. I was relying on the responsible behavior I had seen at the Civic Building. I have worked from the room with you most days over the last two weeks but did not feel I needed to be there full time to supervise you.

I will check in with you on Monday morning. I have a meeting 0900–1030 so will come by after that.

Thank you for the good stats this week. One week to go, so let's make sure we complete the work.

Ciao,

Geraldine

-----Original Message-----
From: Fran
Sent: Fri 26/11/2010 12:44 PM
To: Geraldine
Cc: City
Subject: FW: Shredding Team in Kiwi Room

Geraldine,

Could you please have a word with your team?

Thanks,
Fran

_____

From: Ryan

Sent: Friday, 26 November 2010 12:42 p.m.
To: Fran
Subject: FW: Shredding Team in Kiwi Room

Hi Fran,

Can you please have a word to the team?

Thanks,

Ryan | Commercial & Client Provision Manager
Reserve Agreements, City Council

Please consider the environment before printing this e-mail.

From: Cindy

Sent: Friday, 26 November 2010 12:39 p.m.
To: Ryan
Subject: Shredding Team in Kiwi Room

Hi Ryan,

I understand you look after the shredding team that are currently in residence in the Kiwi Room. My office backs on to this, and there is no sound insulation between the two areas. I've been in twice to ask them to keep the noise down, and Sarah has been in at least once.

It is a bit distracting for me to hear balls bouncing off the walls, along with the bursts of loud cheering.

Sorry to moan about them, but anything you can do?

Cindy

Cindy | Team Leader Ecological Wellbeing

Certifying and Acquiescence - Central

CAUTION: This e-mail memorandum and any attachments holds material that may be private and may be LAWFULLY CONFIDENTIAL. If you are not the planned recipient, any use, revelation, or

71

replication of this memo or attachments is severely forbidden. If you have received this e-mail message in mistake, please inform us directly and remove all duplicates of the memo and attachments. We do not accept accountability for any viruses or alike passed with our e-mail or any properties our e-mail may have on the receiver computer or system. Any opinions conveyed in this e-mail may be those of the specific dispatcher and may not automatically replicate the opinions of Council.

MONDAY, NOVEMBER 29, 2010

In Samoa, after asking, "What's your name? Where are you from?" Most people I met asked, "Do you have kids? Are you married? Do you have a boyfriend?"

I first went to Samoa in June. I was twenty-six, single, and had no children. My lack of love life confused the island. I could only shrug when they asked why. "I just haven't met my husband yet. I don't know where he is, but I know he's not in California. I want to have an adventure, and I'm going to New Zealand next."

Being a hermit all winter in New Zealand, I managed to save up a bit of money. It's cheaper to fly to Samoa from New Zealand than to buy groceries for a week in New Zealand. The small amount I saved was enough money to be able to go back and visit Samoa again in December. I still hadn't met any men, but I had made a platonic friend, Natalie, while working in the basement. We've made an art collective together.

Unfortunately, Natalie gave herself a home haircut before we left for our holiday. She gave herself a mullet. Traveling with a woman with a mullet makes you look like her younger lesbian lover, which I am not. I was single the first time I was in Samoa six months prior, and I was returning to the island with a woman with a mullet.

We were asked by several people, "Are you married?"

Married for over ten years to a very nice man named Phill, Natalie just casually said, "Yes."

After getting questioned about our marital status repeatedly, I explained, "She's married to a man named Phill. I'm single."

The neighbor boy who lived in the house next to the house we were staying in asked if we were married too. And then he asked how old we were and if we had children.

I said to him, "Natalie has a husband. I need a husband before I will think about having a kid."

We were staying with my aunt in a cute house directly across the street from the ocean. The island is gorgeous. There are a lot of wild animals in Samoa. There are community chickens that roam the streets. The baby chicks follow their mama down the street. There are kittens that beg you to drop them a scrap of food at restaurants everywhere. There are sea turtles that pop their heads out of the water and seem to say hello. Fruit bats fly overhead, from treetop to treetop.

The island also has wild dogs that roam the streets. The dogs are filthy, mangy mutts with gimp legs from being hit by cars, patches of fur missing, engorged tumors, and fleas, but they're honestly the happiest-looking dogs in the world. They look like they're smiling because they're free to roam the beautiful island and eat whatever they can find on the street, with an ocean view and no owner scolding them. They sleep in the gutters, with cars driving by inches from them, without flinching. They sincerely seem content and happy, almost arrogantly happy to be free.

Before returning to the island, my aunt told me that she had rescued a dog she found on the street and had named him Fatu, which means "heart" in Samoan. I cringed at the news; I was expecting what I had seen in the streets the first time I was in Samoa. The thought of sharing a house with a stray street dog might put a damper on my island getaway.

I was pleasantly surprised to meet Fatu. He was an adorable, sweet, mild-mannered puppy with soft, blonde fur and large green eyes. My aunt found him at a bus stop across the street from the house. The neighborhood kids told her, "Why don't you take him home since you are a doctor. He has leprosy."

Fatu didn't have leprosy, just mange. He was super skinny when she found him and had been hit by two cars. Both his back legs were mangled, and he walked on three legs. Despite his gimpy legs, he was still adorable and lovable.

Fatu wasn't tough enough for the street life. He exuded

absolute gratitude for being adopted by my aunt. He never begged for food while we ate, he never jumped on people, and he rarely barked. He was still a puppy, yet much better behaved than most pampered pooches I've met. We would take him on walks; he was content on the leash and did his best to run on three legs.

Fatu's legs that had been hit by multiple cars were beginning to swell from infection. Samoa doesn't have veterinarian clinics. There's no place to take injured animals on the island. There is someone who is a trained vet with family on the island, which she visits occasionally. Luckily for Fatu, she was on the island while we were vacationing.

While we walked him, other street dogs would follow. They would sniff him and get in his face. They looked arrogant and like they were making fun of him for being on a leash, laughing at him for not being free like them. When the dogs would bully him, Fatu would look back at us with big, pleading, puppy-dog eyes.

On our walk, we passed the bus stop where he was rescued. He sat down at the bus stop and let out a heartfelt howl as if saying, "This is where I was found."

We made it to the pharmacy, trying to guess which house across from it the vet lived in. There aren't numbers on the houses in Samoa. There's a post office across the street from the museum, where everyone goes and collects their mail. After knocking on a few wrong doors and avoiding getting attacked by a pack of wild dogs, we ended up buying a handful of syringes filled with mange medicine in the street from a Samoan lady.

TUESDAY, NOVEMBER 30, 2010

Other than buying syringes in the streets, we did touristy things, like snorkeling, sightseeing, and drinking piña coladas at Tisa's Barefoot Bar. Tisa's is my favorite bar in the entire world, and she makes the best piña coladas.

In one of the villages in Samoa, there's a legend that if children of the village sing a song, the turtle and the shark come to the surface of the water.

This time, I didn't see Junior, the giant Samoan man who is almost seven feet tall, over three hundred pounds, and covered in tattoos, with a teardrop tattoo on his face, and whom I had to pay five dollars to sing. When I was here in June, within two minutes of Junior and his friends singing, a turtle and a shark surfaced together, and as soon as the singing stopped, they went away.

This time, there were about six Samoan teenagers who sang, and I only saw a turtle, no shark. When they finished singing, I asked them, "Do you know Junior? When I was here in June, the turtle and the shark popped right up."

Alarmed, they all looked around at each other and didn't answer my Junior inquiry. The island is only twenty miles in length, so I'm sure everyone knows everyone in Samoa, and they must know Junior. I thought a description may help, "You know Junior? Big, tall guy with a teardrop tattoo?"

"You know Big T?"

"If he's from this village and sings the turtle and the shark song, yeah, I think so."

"He's with the police. They got him. He shot someone."

Not sure exactly how to respond, I said, "Well, when I was here in June, he was really nice. And when he sang, the turtle and shark popped right up out of the water."

They looked at me like I suddenly had Samoan street cred. They all introduced themselves and shook my hand and said I could stay in their village as long as I wanted.

SUNDAY, DECEMBER 5, 2010

The guys I lived with didn't clean the house at all while I was in Samoa. I was only gone a week, but the place was in shambles. Not only had the garbage not been taken out, there were bags and bags of new garbage in piles around the overflowing garbage can. All of the dishes were dirty and piled around the kitchen.

Months ago, I started using my shampoo as body wash when I found a hair that was not mine on my soap. I stopped buying bars of soap and continued washing my body with my shampoo. They never replaced the bar of soap or bought themselves new bars of soap. I would find the hand soap in the shower a lot of the time, so I assume that's what they were using to wash themselves.

I just cut a clove of garlic with a pair of scissors and tried to scramble an egg in a pot because all the dishes are dirty. I really have been living with boys for too long.

TUESDAY, DECEMBER 7, 2010

There's a man who's bald and wears a toupee to work every day at my new job. He only wears it in the morning and takes it off in the afternoon. He says it keeps his head warm. He's a little Asian man, and the toupee looks like something an Elvis impersonator would wear.

That temp job ticking boxes on a piece of paper was directly one floor above the office I'm in now. When I was one floor up ticking boxes and removing staples, we got scolded for playing ball too loudly inside.

The deck inspections team leader came into the shredding team's office. I thought we were getting in trouble, but she came in and said she heard we were a hardworking team, wanting all of our resumes to offer us jobs as deck inspections administrators when our contracts were up. That's how I got my job: bouncing a ball loudly one floor above the office I'm in now.

WEDNESDAY, DECEMBER 8, 2010

The people at my new job are really strange. The hyperactive Kiwi guy named Bob in the cubicle next to me told me that he wrote and performed a play called A Day in the Life of Lentini. Bob told me lentini means "the silent one" in Italian. He wrote a silent story about a mime, which he performed in front of an audience of fifty people.

I laughed, "What was there to write if it was a silent performance?"

Bob stood up in his cubicle and started miming at me.

He's thirty-six and single but does a lot of online dating. He still lives at home with his parents and sleeps in a single bed. He has a shiny, round, bald head and wears thick glasses over his small, beady eyes. He has a manic laugh— the type you would hear the villain have in a horror movie. His cubicle is clean and covered in perfectly straight, laminated pictures of soccer players and Kim Kardashian. And he's a mime. He talks nonstop all day.

I told him, "You're the world's loudest mime."

THURSDAY, DECEMBER 9, 2010

Bob puts sunscreen on his bald head, unlike the other strange man I work with who wears a toupee outside and takes it off inside the office. Bob put a lot of sunscreen on his head today—so much that his round, bald head glistened.

A lady noticed the shiny bald head from across the office.

She came up close to him and said, "Wow, your head is so shiny. How did you get it to shine like that?"

I told him, "You look like a puppet from Sesame Street, like you should be a bald friend of Bert and Ernie."

Is there To Catch a Predator down here? It's a TV show where they catch pedophiles. If there were a puppet version of To Catch a Predator, he would be a puppet they would catch. He is like the bald, perverted friend of Bert and Ernie.

FRIDAY, DECEMBER 10, 2010

I moved into a small cottage in a back garden by myself in Grey Lynn. Grey Lynn is just a bit farther away from the city center than Ponsonby. It's an artsy-looking neighborhood and more down to earth than Ponsonby.

There was something with claws running all over the roof of my cottage last night. I hope it was a wild cat or possum. It sounded like a velociraptor was on my roof all night, trying to claw its way through my roof to eat me alive. I seem to primarily live in cottages with wild cats on the roof.

At the last place I lived in California, all the neighborhood cats in heat liked to use my roof as their mating-call headquarters. I had never heard a cat in heat before. I thought there was an injured baby in my yard and went outside to rescue it. I looked up and saw two cats making weird noises on my roof, slowly following each other around. I threw rocks near them, not to hit them, just to scare them off my roof. It was the middle of the night, and they were keeping me awake. I shouted at the cats trying to get some, "I'm not getting any either. Go away!"

SUNDAY, DECEMBER 12, 2010

I was chanting at a Buddhist's house this afternoon with about half a dozen young women in their twenties who live in Auckland. Since it's summer and hot now, we were chanting with the door open. As we chanted, a little old islander man peered his head in the open door and looked as if he had seen a ghost. He said, "Are you Buddhists?"

"Yes, come on in."

We introduced ourselves; his name is Jim.

"Wow, I started chanting in the 70s, but I haven't done it for a while. I didn't know there were Buddhists in town," Jim said.

I said, "It seems like there is a Buddhist chanting on every block in Auckland. Where do you live? I'm sure there is one near you."

"I'm way over in Grey Lynn."

"That's where I live! What street are you on?" I asked.

"Wellplace."

"That's my street! I'm in a cottage behind number eleven."

"I'm at three," he smiled.

"There's another Buddhist who lives around the corner from me. I chant with her every morning before work."

"Vicky?"

"Yeah, you know her?"

"We go way back," he smiled. "Can I go with you tomorrow morning and surprise her?"

FRIDAY, DECEMBER 17, 2010

Jim, Vicky, and I have been chanting together before I go to work every morning this week, from six to seven. Vicky was so excited to see him. They both know I'm chanting for a boyfriend, and Jim jokes, "She's chanting for a boyfriend, and she got me instead."

I started chanting Nam Myoho Renge Kyo for my heart to be open to the right person. I'm chanting that 2011 is my year to meet my husband. It felt like something shifted in me, in my chest—an opening feeling. It's scary for me to be vulnerable. This practice is Buddhism in everyday life; it doesn't require celibacy or my monkish behavior.

SATURDAY, DECEMBER 18, 2010

I had been having a nice, quiet morning drinking tea and slowly waking up by myself in my cottage. I thought a little yoga might be nice to do. I picked up my yoga mat, and there was a huge cockroach on it. I screamed, almost started crying, and threw the yoga mat on the ground. I opened the front door, hoping the cockroach would wander outside on its own. It hasn't. I e-mailed my dad about the cockroach. He lives in Georgia and can't help.

Fifteen minutes after staring at my now cockroach-tainted yoga mat, I was planning to throw the yoga mat outside. The cockroach didn't stay on it. It started running, but away from the door instead of out the door. I screamed bloodcurdling squeals, jumped up and down, and then hit it with a dustpan several times. The cockroach went from crunchy to squishy and juicy.

It's very dead and outside now.

I'm still shaking. I'm not comforted by the fact that I can scream hysterically on multiple occasions before eleven in the morning and my neighbors don't notice. My throat hurts from screaming.

MONDAY, DECEMBER 20, 2010

I watched the Christmas Monologues written and directed by Thomas Sainsbury. Roberto Nascimento was once again my favorite performance, playing a perverted Santa.

Thomas Sainsbury asked me to write and perform a monologue for him in his upcoming play, The Foreign Monologues. I've never ever done anything like that before. He seemed amused by my manic behavior and giggling description of the shitty temp jobs I've been doing since arriving in New Zealand.

Whenever I'm in his proximity, I'm so nervous I can't stop laughing or talking. I can't prevent myself from telling him every dirty little secret I have. He smiles and looks at me closely, as if examining me with his green eyes that seem to go through me. I can't tell if he is amused or horrified; there seems to be a mix of attraction and repulsion chemistry coming from him. Sometimes he stares so closely that I think he's about to kiss me; other times he looks like he wants to put duct tape over my mouth.

After describing working in a basement that smelled like rotten cabbage and being told by my boss, "You don't need to pretend to be nice, you will never get a raise," Tom asked, "Has anyone ever told you you're funny?"

I told my grandma that the most prolific playwright in New Zealand wants me to write and perform a monologue for him. My grandma's response was, "Well, your family certainly likes to laugh at you. If you tell him about your ex-boyfriends, he will be sure to laugh his head off."

Thanks for the encouragement, Grandma.

FRIDAY, DECEMBER 24, 2010

At work there's a secret Santa gift exchange. I started the job too late to be in it. There's a creepy, cross-eyed, fat guy with a missing tooth dressed up as Santa and handing out gifts in the cubicle across the room. I think guys dressed as Santa are almost as creepy as clowns.

Bob the mime told me, "Last Christmas, at the work holiday party, the last temp and I got drunk and fucked on the desk you're sitting at now."

"Well, that's definitely not going to happen this year with me."

Bob got a card with a lotto ticket in it. The card cover had a nativity scene with a baby Jesus that looked about seven years old. The seven-year-old baby Jesus had an arrogant smirk on his face, like, "That's right, I'm the son of God." Above the nativity scene, "Joyous Christmas Greetings" was written in gold script.

The inside read, "May peace and joy of Christmas be with you today and always." Bob's secret Santa crossed out Christmas and wrote "God." The card said, "May the peace and joy of God be with you today and always."

Bob's secret Santa also wrote, "Don't forget the reason for the season is…"

Bob asked me, "Do you go to church?"

"Actually, I go to a Buddhist center. I practice Buddhism."

"You're not really Buddhist."

"No, really, I chant Nam Myoho Renge Kyo."

"Huh?"

"Nam Myoho Renge Kyo. Basically, being Buddhist is just

taking responsibility for your life; the word karma means action, so to change your karma you have to change your actions. A Buddha is just a human being awakened to their own potential. Everyone has the potential for Buddhahood. When I chant, I'm not chanting to anything outside myself, just to bring forth the Buddha from within. Chanting makes me feel happy."

"Whatever, I drink beer for that."

A few moments later, everyone in the office received an e-mail with the "Jingle Bells" song. First Bob opened the e-mail.

I said, "No! Shut it down!"

Bob responded, "Oh good, it just repeats when the song ends."

One cubicle after another, they all opened the e-mail at different times, and "Jingle Bells" was playing on a dozen different computers but seconds out of sync from each other.

Then people started singing along to "Jingle Bells," and one person said, "Who needs a radio when you can sing Christmas carols?"

I almost started crying in my cubicle. I am not meant for the cubicle life.

SUNDAY, DECEMBER 26, 2010

Council is closed from Christmas until January 5. It's nice to have some time off. Yesterday I spent Christmas with Natalie and Phill. Natalie and Phill have such an amazing marriage; they've been together for over ten years and are each other's best friend.

We just walked their dogs and relaxed in their back garden. They took me on a little train ride called the Rainforest Express that went through glowworm caves in the Waitakere Ranges. The views from the train are dreamlike. I'm not sure if it's because of the hole in the ozone, but all the colors here seem more intense, like looking through polarized lenses. I see rainbows almost every day. New Zealand really is a beautiful country.

MONDAY, JANUARY 3, 2011

New Year's Eve I watched the fireworks with my friend Lily in the Auckland Viaduct. Lily invited other people to watch the fireworks too. At nearly the stroke of midnight, I heard the sexiest accent I've ever heard in the dark. Out of the dark night emerged a handsome blond man who's friends with Lily. I could feel him watching me as the fireworks went off overhead. I stole glances at him out of the corner of my eye.

His name is Grant. He's single, Scottish, and lives a couple streets away from me. He was chain-smoking all night. After finding out we're neighbors, he asked me out for neighborly tea. I didn't give him my phone number the first time he asked. I'm not sure about him. He's really cute, but I don't want to date a smoker. He said he's quitting.

I went to the Coromandel Bay over the weekend with Lily. It was beautiful there. We stayed in a hostel that was a converted schoolhouse. It was close to the beach, where we spent most of our time.

The first night in Coromandel, Lily and I wrote down New Year's resolutions at midnight, and we threw them in the bonfire. I'm scared to open up and be vulnerable, but I don't want to be in heartbreak hibernation anymore.

SUNDAY, JANUARY 9, 2011

I had neighborly tea with Grant yesterday. We met at the Gypsy Tea Room in Grey Lynn. He got there before me. I heard he's divorced and a bit older. He doesn't have the year of his birth on Facebook, just the date January 13. He only has a few pictures of himself too, hiking in Scotland. He looks equally handsome and haunted in them.

Grant wore strange, baggy linen clothes that don't fit him very well. One of my friends in California is divorced and lost all of her money. He looks broke but has these giant blue eyes that I get lost in. I really don't know very much about Scotland. He told me stories about his grandpa, who was from the Highlands of Scotland and a bit psychic. The sun was to his back as he spoke, making his blond hair glow like a halo. He's otherworldly looking, like an elf from Lord of the Rings.

Grant rolls his Rs when he talks. His accent is the sexiest I've ever heard. Grant ran his own gardening and garden-design business in Scotland and now works at a garden center in Auckland. As we went on a long walk around Auckland, he told me the Latin words for plants, rolling his Rs. I had no idea what he was saying, but I didn't care. I couldn't get over how sexy he sounded and how eccentrically handsome he is—he mesmerized me.

He's chewing nicotine gum now; he swears he's quitting smoking. He ended up buying me dinner, and he nervously asked how old I was. He seemed relieved when I told him I was twenty-seven. He said I looked a lot younger. He's turning thirty-four on the thirteenth.

I wore flip-flop sandals (called "jandals" here) that I bought for one dollar. They kept falling apart when we walked. It was really embarrassing.

At the end of the night, I didn't know what to do. About a block from my house, I said, "I have to go now," and I walked away really quickly.

Grant looked a bit insulted and confused. "OK, see you later."

TUESDAY, JANUARY 11, 2011

I shouldn't have acted so awkward with Grant. Why did I run away? I think I might like him. I haven't heard from him. I'm such an idiot.

WEDNESDAY, JANUARY 12, 2011

This morning while I ate an orange, Bob the mime said, "I would like to drink your blood because it probably tastes sweet because you eat so much fruit." He continued with a manic laugh, "If I cut off your arm with a machete, orange juice would pour out."

It was half past eight in the morning. I'm not a morning person and became aware at this moment that I hadn't drank enough coffee before I arrived at work. I continued to eat my orange silently, unable to respond. Then he noticed I was wearing shoes instead of sandals and said, "You're wearing Chuck Taylors today. I can't tickle your feet."

I said, "Yes, I know, I wore them on purpose for that reason."

Bob's been sneaking up behind me and tickling my feet. I kick him when he does it, but he doesn't stop. I managed to leave the office without having my blood sucked or my feet tickled by a mime.

THURSDAY, JANUARY 13, 2011

There's another pregnant lady at work, and she was really hoping to have a boy, but she's having a girl. When she came back to work after she found out the news, she told everyone she was disappointed. I tried to comfort her, I said, "Maybe your baby will grow up to be a lesbian."

All the heads in the cubicles turned toward me with big eyes and a few dropped jaws. I smiled and went back to work.

A few hours later, she was talking to someone else who had a more office appropriate response; they said, "Maybe she'll be a tomboy."

FRIDAY, JANUARY 14, 2011

Yesterday was Grant's birthday. He invited a group of people in the Global Work Abroad Network out to drinks. In order to save up to go out for his birthday, I had to eat oatmeal for breakfast, lunch, and dinner. He's so much cuter than I remember. This was the first time I've seen him since neighborly tea. I could feel him staring at me from across the table. At the end of the night, he walked me to my bus stop and kissed me on the cheek. It made me want him to kiss me on the lips.

MONDAY, JANUARY 17, 2011

If there was a disease caused by working in cubicles, it would be called cubicleitous. I've got it bad. Humans are not meant to be in cubicles. Antsy does not begin to describe it. I cannot believe they are playing Hootie and the Blowfish anywhere in the world still. The only thing keeping me sane is having my desk at a window. I would jump out, but I'm on the first floor.

I tried going on a walk to Victoria Park, where there's a

track, on my lunch break. It's next to a lot of office buildings. A lot of cubicle people in gray office clothes walk in circles around the track. Walking in circles with cubicle people made me have a panic attack. I feel like a hamster on a wheel.

THURSDAY, JANUARY 20, 2011

Grant took me out on a date. We went on a long walk around Grey Lynn. We ended up getting pizza.

He told me one of his coworkers was thinking of ways to get rich. He wanted to buy a McDonald's and a brothel. According to Grant's coworker, you just have to register your whore at the post office to become a pimp.

Grant's coworker wants to combine the two businesses and call it McBrothel. If they did, would it have a drive-through where you could order a Happy Meal with a happy ending?

I would be very reluctant to ask for special sauce on my Big Mac at McBrothel. Can french-fry grease be used as lube? Could you order the golden arches if you wanted a golden shower? What would the uniforms be at McBrothel? Would they cater to those with a clown fetish? Let Ronald McDonald turn your frown upside down. What's the real reason he wears gloves?

I want to see the menu at McBrothel. What comes with a Sausage McMuffin or a Quarter Pounder? For the health conscious, McBrothel is now serving tossed salads.

McBrothel would be the ultimate gluttonous/lustful fantasy.

SUNDAY, JANUARY 22, 2011

It took me a couple of months of cutting back to save up for a laptop. After eating oatmeal for at least two meals a day for a couple of months to save up, I was finally able to buy a laptop that was on sale. I had been paying for Internet in my cottage, with no way to use it. The blinking lights of the Wi-Fi setup had been taunting me. I brought my shiny new laptop home, and the first thing I did was check my e-mail. The first e-mail in my in-box was a notification from my US bank stating my account was overdrawn. I need to figure out how to pinch pennies harder.

TUESDAY, JANUARY 25, 2011

Our first kiss was a bit awkward. It was really dark, and we couldn't see each other's faces. He kissed me on the lips, but it seemed like an accident. After he kissed me on the lips, Grant kissed me on the cheek. We stared at each other, and he gave me another quick kiss on the lips.

Then he said, "Umm, I have to wake up early to work in the morning. Need to go."

"Yeah, me too. Thanks again for dinner."

"Do you fancy a catch-up this weekend?"

"That would be nice."

After he left, I panicked. What if he wasn't trying to kiss my lips and I made him kiss my lips?

I sent him a panicked text, apologizing for the awkward kiss:

> It was nice to see you. Sorry I was awkward kissing you good night on lips when you were aiming for the cheek. Sorry about that. Thanks again for dinner. Always nice to walk and talk with you.

He sent a text message a few minutes later:

> Ha ha. No problem. Was aiming for the lips myself but couldn't see in the dark. Nice to see you, sorry if I was awkward. How about a catch-up this weekend. Have a lovely day tomorrow. Take care.

WEDNESDAY, JANUARY 26, 2011

My job is booking deck inspections. I receive calls requesting deck inspections. I try not to laugh when I have Kiwis, who pronounce E as I, calling about their decks.

"Yes, I need my deck inspected."

"I need to get my deck waterproofed."

"I need the foundation of my deck inspected."

"I got a new deck, can someone come look at it?"

94

"I had an inspection done on my hanging deck."

"I need a cavity inspection for my deck."

"Do you do inspections for deck connections?"

Sometimes customers are vague about what type of inspection they need on their deck, so I'm forced to ask, "What type of inspection do you need for your deck?"

Yesterday a man with a smooth and sultry radio voice called wanting me to look at the history of his deck-inspection records. I informed him, "It looks like back in 1999, you had an inspection done on a large, hanging deck extending from a bedroom."

"Oh really?" the smooth voice said, "It says in your notes that an inspection was done on a large hanging deck extending from my bedroom?"

THURSDAY, JANUARY 27, 2011

Bob the mime asked me if I brought a gun with me to New Zealand. I sarcastically said, "Yeah, you want to see it," and reached for my purse. He jumped back, believing I had a gun. "I'm joking, why would I have a gun with me?"

"You're American. I thought all Americans had guns and brought them with them everywhere they went."

SATURDAY, JANUARY 29, 2011

I think Grant and I are dating now. We're both so awkward and pale. I trust him because he seems to be more clueless about dating than me. I'm too nervous to let him sit down in my house because I'm afraid of what might happen. I only sit with him in public places, like park benches. I think he's broke; he has duct tape and staples holding his shoes together.

It's really hot. With the lack of ozone in New Zealand, we're getting sunburned, even with a hundred SPF on. We had lunch the other day, and after I asked what Grant wanted to do next, he said, "I'm really hot and tired, I just want to sit down."

"OK, let's go to the Auckland Domain. You can sit on a park bench there."

He just sighs and sits politely on park benches next to me and holds my hand. It feels like old-school Sense and Sensibility courtship.

Last night, Grant had made me dinner at his house. His hands were shaking nervously while cutting veggies for a stir-fry. We listened to music on YouTube while he cooked. I asked him what music he likes, and I thought he said The Whores, so I searched for them on YouTube. I played the first video. Grant looked confused, stopped cooking, and walked to the other side of the kitchen to look at the computer screen. He blushed, "Let me type it in for you." He typed, "The Horrors." His Scottish accent made it sound like The Whores to my ears.

"Sorry, I thought that was a strange name for a band but just thought it was a Scottish band I had never heard of."

After dinner we had a few kisses, and then he said, "You can spend the night, but I'm afraid I might take advantage of you."

I laughed, "I'm definitely going home tonight."

We have to work on kissing before thinking about sleepovers. He walked me home and held my hand. I think I intimidate him. He's really nervous, and we've only had a few awkward kisses. He gives me little pecks and says, "I need to remember how to kiss."

SUNDAY, JANUARY 30, 2011

Grant and I were at Rangitoto Island, and a giant bumblebee landed on my neck. He gently said, "There's a little bug on you" and reached for it.

I felt a huge, furry creature on me, so I jumped and started screaming hysterically at the top of my lungs and spinning in circles. It was a very hot day, and I had made the mistake of wearing a wool sweater for an all-day hike on a black lava–covered island, and I was bright red and covered in sweat. I looked like a scene from the Exorcist. I don't know why he continued to ask me out after this.

I screamed so loud Grant jumped back startled. He tried to calm me with his sweet, Scottish accent, "Shh, shh, it's OK, you're all right. It flew away. It won't hurt you." It probably sounded like someone was chopping me up with an axe.

After I recovered from the bumblebee, we walked around the rest of the island. As we walked, he kept trying to hold my hand. Grant packed us sandwiches for lunch. He said, "I didn't know what you like, so I made five different types of sandwiches."

When we got back on the boat to go back to Auckland, it was really windy, and he said, "Burr," rolling his Rs. I think I'll stop running away from him.

TUESDAY, FEBRUARY 1, 2011

After an art show, I was drunk and kept kissing Grant as he walked me home. I was pressing myself up against him, and he kept leaning back, being polite. When you kiss American guys, they press themselves up against you; Scottish guys apparently don't.

Grant said, "I need to remember how to woo the ladies. I have to go home." He gave me tiny kisses and ran away into the night.

WEDNESDAY, FEBRUARY 2, 2011

I had a meeting about accreditation and the merging of the councils creating the super city. I was informed by an anonymous upper management man who reminded me of an alpha-male silverback gorilla in a suit that "accreditation is important because, during World War II, the Americans were sold guns that didn't work, and we all know that Americans love their guns."

He continued his pep talk by stating, "You are all tools." With a long pause, he looked around the room at bored cubicle people. Some that were asleep. "In a system," he continued, "at Council. You are like monkeys running on barrels, and you need to make sure you don't fall off the barrel!"

Thanks for the inspiration, sir; I'll take that back to my cubicle. That guy was a tool, not me. As he was leaving the room, I tapped him on the arm and whispered sweetly in his ear with a smile, "Just to let you know, not all Americans love guns, most people I know hate them."

I might be making peanuts, but I'm no monkey.

SATURDAY, FEBRUARY 5, 2011

I'm still getting used to being in a relationship again and keeping in touch with someone. Early this week, Grant told me he had an allergic reaction to peanuts and had to go to the emergency room. I hadn't heard from him in a couple of days and then remembered this was the last I had heard from him. I sent him a text to make sure he was all right. He's fine, despite my neglect.

MONDAY, FEBRUARY 7, 2011

I heard another international temp say she was temping during the election and processing the votes. She pressed the 'Enter' button on the keyboard for three weeks straight. On the last day, she had to press the 'Enter' button from eight in the morning to ten at night on a Saturday.

TUESDAY, FEBRUARY 8, 2011

Grant is so sweet. He always says he's going to turn into a pumpkin when it gets late. He's so gentle, considerate, and respectful with me. He really makes me feel like a lady. I feel so calm about him, which is abnormal for me. We held hands and went on a long walk around Western Springs and then to the Wintergarden Pavilion in the Auckland Domain. I was wearing one hundred SPF, but I'm super sunburned. After our walk, we cuddled and watched a zombie TV show he downloaded. He wants to take me on a road trip in two weeks. I like him a lot. He's nice to cuddle next to. Grant kisses me good night gently.

SATURDAY, FEBRUARY 12, 2011

Last night I went to farewell drinks for a friend going back home to Japan. The topic of baby names came up among us girls. I said, "I want to name a girl Zuiki. I hear it means 'joyful acceptance' in Japanese. Is that true?"

"Zuiki?" my Japanese friend Kana asked. "No, that sounds

like the Japanese word for beans."

SUNDAY, FEBRUARY 13, 2011

Grant places his hands on my shoulders or the small of my
back so gently, as if he is afraid he's going to break me. We
have been going on lots of walks and holding hands. He
keeps telling me, "I need to remember how to woo the
ladies."

I'm wooed already, and he can't figure it out.

TUESDAY, FEBRUARY 15, 2011

I picked Grant flowers from gardens in my neighborhood.
I wasn't sure if we would be celebrating Valentine's Day or
not. He came over to fix my sink. He saw the Valentine's
cards my Grandma and mom sent me and got jealous and
asked who they were from.

He said, "I feel like a jerk showing up on Valentine's Day
with a hammer and a spanner."

I realized it was Valentine's Day on my way home from
work after I passed a bunch of closed shops that had
Valentine's displays in their window.

I told him, "I spent the last two Valentine's Days single
and working in the floral department. You're thoughtful
and considerate for fixing my sink for me."

THURSDAY, FEBRUARY 17, 2011

At eight this morning, I was leaning on the coffee machine, waiting for my mug to be filled with cheap coffee to get my caffeine fix. An old man in the office saw me leaning on the coffee machine and asked, "Are you Irish?"

"Yeah, I'm part Irish."

"Which part of Ireland are you from?"

"No, I just have Irish ancestry. I'm from California—a small town north of San Francisco."

"Where's your California suntan?"

"I have never had a tan in my life. I burn and freckle. End of story."

He was annoyingly peppy at this hour. I grabbed my mug and walked away from him to the fridge, filled the rest of the cup with cold milk, and began chugging my coffee as I do every morning.

"I saw in the paper that California has a lot of litter. It's not Reagan's California anymore, is it?"

"Reagan was elected before I was born."

He continued to ramble about Reagan as I chugged my coffee unresponsively.

SATURDAY, FEBRUARY 19, 2011

Grant texted me that he was lying in bed and tickety boo. I had never heard of tickety boo, so I assumed it meant tired. I texted back, "Sorry to keep you up. I'll let you sleep. If tickety boo means tired, I am tickety boo too, good night."

He texted back, "Tickety boo means doing all right."

Grant says "aye" for "yes," and "wee" is in every sentence: "You're just a wee flower."

Another time he said something that I heard wrong was when he said he did an "order for plants" at his job working in the garden center. I thought he said an "orgy with plants." He laughed when I told him that and said, "Yes, I really like lettuce."

I feel like I need two dictionaries now: Kiwi English to American English and Scottish English to American English.

SUNDAY, FEBRUARY 20, 2011

Lily and I were assistants at a show my old flatmate Liam was in. It was a water ballet called Sirens, and he played a guy who was lured into the water by the sirens' singing. It was an amazing show. Liam did a great job; he really stood out among the rest of the male actors.

MONDAY, FEBRUARY 21, 2011

Bob the mime wanted to buy panty hose for this girl he's seeing, but he didn't want to look like a weirdo buying them and asked me to go with him to the store. I thought the fresh air would be nice, so we walked to a local department store on our lunch break. When we got to the store, he said he needed crotch-less panty hose. I freaked out and told him no.

TUESDAY, FEBRUARY 22, 2011

There was another huge earthquake in Christchurch. That place won't stop shaking. A lot of people died this time.

Mobile phones all over New Zealand aren't working.

WEDNESDAY, FEBRUARY 23, 2011

Today Bob asked if I wanted to tag along with him while he went to buy small scissors to trim his nose hair. I declined.

THURSDAY, FEBRUARY 24, 2011

Bob the mime with the bald head was making fun of my hair and then starting singing, "I sniff glue every day!"

I asked, "What time is it?" He responded, "It's fuck o'clock."

While I was eating fruit and a blueberry bran muffin, he said, "I'm on the I'm-trying-to-kill-myself diet. I have a pixie bar, bag of chips, and a fizzy drink."

Once I bought a donut. Bob ate my donut; he shoved the whole thing in his mouth and left a trail of sugar all over the ground. I said, "Look, mime tracks."

FRIDAY, FEBRUARY 25, 2011

Bob has pills he takes every morning. He has trouble taking the lid off the pill bottle. It makes a horrible noise, like cracking knuckles.

I asked, "What are you taking?"

"Crazy pills."

SUNDAY, FEBRUARY 27, 2011

We went to the lantern festival over the weekend, and I ate a piece of barbecued meat that I think made me sick. I've had a fever all weekend and just wanted to sleep. I'm still burning up. I e-mailed my mom, who's a nurse. I don't know what to do. I have never had a fever for so long. My head, neck, and back have been hurting so badly, and I'm still coughing, and my chest hurts. If you don't have residency in New Zealand, it costs a hundred dollars to see a doctor, not including prescriptions. I really can't afford that.

105

Grant came by my place and brought me grapes and Manuka honey. He couldn't call or text me because our phones still aren't working after the earthquake, so I had my glasses on instead of contacts, and looked like a sick nerd. He's really sweet to me.

MONDAY, FEBRUARY 28, 2011

When Bob returned from his lunch break, he said, "I watch the world go by on my lunch break," while bobbing his head, like watching boobs, then his eyes went down, like looking at a butt. "So, with the front view I look here," he said while pointing to his chest. "With the back view, I look here," he said while pointing to his butt.

I have become numb to hearing stories such as this.

TUESDAY, MARCH 1, 2011

Grant's planning to take me on a road trip around the northern tip of the North Island next weekend. I've never dated a guy who made plans like this. It's awesome. He's calling it a Magical Mystery Tour. On Saturday night we'll be staying in Whangarei District, on Sunday either near Bay of Islands or around The Far North, and on Monday Opononi and Omapere. The girls at my work are jealous. One said, "Wow, you're dating a real man, not a boy."

THURSDAY, MARCH 3, 2011

This morning, before getting in the car for our road trip, Grant tried to pull his car into the driveway because it was pouring with rain. He came up to the door where I was waiting and said, "I can't pull into your tight entrance."

I smiled, and he blushed. I think I really like this man.

FRIDAY, MARCH 4, 2011

Last night we stayed at Little Earth Lodge outside Whangarei. It was really cute and reminded me of a hobbit shire. A lot of the towns in New Zealand are Maori words that we have no idea how to pronounce. As copilot trying to guide Grant as he drives, I'm spelling words out, and we try to guess how to say towns and streets. In the Maori language, Wh is pronounced as an F. The whole drive up to Whangarei, Grant repeated the name Whangarei, attempting to say it correctly with an F. He's very sweet, but I'm glad to leave Whangarei, just so I don't have to hear the name again.

Grant bought a used, teal Subaru station wagon. It's the type of car a mom would drive in America. He drives really slowly.

SATURDAY, MARCH 5, 2011

We went to the Ninety Mile Beach and tried to climb up a giant sand dune to get to the beach. It was really windy, and we didn't make it over the sand dune. I was completely covered in sand: it was on my scalp; in my ears, eyes, and nose; and all over my skin. I wore a dress and thong underwear and got sand in there too.

Getting back in the car after the sand dune, it was really uncomfortable to sit in a sandy thong. I apologized to Grant, "Sorry, this isn't very ladylike, but I really need to take off my underwear." He looked a bit startled but excited as he drove and I squirmed out of my undies in his passenger seat.

There aren't a lot of restaurants up here, so we've been getting food from Pak'n Save, a really cheap, poorly lit warehouse-style grocery store where you bag your own groceries. We ended up in a Pak'n Save in a random small town. Grant was worried about leaving his car in the parking lot. Inside, most people seemed to be missing teeth, and lots of people had rattail hairstyles or mullets.

We ended up in the freezer aisle, and I whispered to Grant, "We should get what we need and go as soon as possible. I feel really weird in here without underwear on."

SUNDAY, MARCH 6, 2011

We went to Cape Reinga, the most northern point in New Zealand, and saw where the Pacific Ocean meets the Tasman Sea. It's weird that it creates a wave where the ocean and sea meet.

Grant took me to the Puketiti Lodge in Mangonui. I was

totally shocked; it was the nicest place I've ever stayed. It was on top of a hill, and there were amazing views of the sea. We laid on the bed and watched the sunset. I bit my tongue, trying not to say "I love you" for the first time. I'm afraid to say it first; I'm afraid he won't say it back.

At night there were shooting stars. We walked on the back deck to watch them. It wasn't very well lit, and Grant missed the step down to the deck and fell on the ground. We both laughed as I helped him up off the ground. It was then that I knew I really was in love with him. I love him. I would totally marry him.

MONDAY, MARCH 7, 2011

Grant spent the night with me when we got back from our road trip. I'm still chanting every morning at six with my neighbors Jim and Vicky before work. I really need to chant before work to prepare me for the day. I woke up at half past five to get ready. It was still dark when I left the house. Grant said, "You Buddhists sure do wake up early."

WEDNESDAY, MARCH 9, 2011

Grant's so sweet and polite. He's always like, "Oh dear" or "Oh dearie" instead of swearing, while I'm constantly saying, "Fuck!"

We went to a friend's girlfriend's burlesque show that was very G-rated; they mainly were hula hooping. During the show, Grant mumbled something, and I asked him to repeat what he said,

He said, "I can't say something vulgar in polite company."

"Who's the polite company?" I asked while looking around to see who he was talking about.

Grant looked at me with the world's bluest eyes, his baby-soft, pale skin and silky, platinum-blond hair as innocent as a baby lamb and softly said with his sexy Scottish accent, "You're the polite company."

I have never encountered a gentleman before and have no idea how to respond to one. I'm from California; I'm used to flipping guys off in the street and telling them to go fuck themselves and to stop following me. I'm a small girl—you have to be twice as tough when you're pint size. I hope I don't scare him away with my vulgarity. Maybe I will turn into a lady with him and stop swearing like a sailor.

Mirror, mirror on the wall, he is the fairest of them all.

THURSDAY, MARCH 10, 2011

Grant was mumbling with his Scottish accent in his sleep, and I couldn't understand him. In the morning there were really loud crickets. He said, "It's like the Amazon."

I thought he said, "I'd like a banana." So I responded, "Are you hungry? I have bananas."

SATURDAY, MARCH 12, 2011

Maybe because I'm getting older or just boring, but these days I find it more exciting to stay in and get a good night's sleep than to stay out. I keep old-lady hours. My friend Lily and Grant have both woken me up when trying to get in touch with me at ten at night. Whenever that happens, I'm so dead asleep that I think it's morning and almost start making coffee to start my day. I go to the phone before I start make coffee, thinking it's the alarm clock I have on my phone, only to discover it's not the alarm, it's a text message or my phone's ringing. Grant was worried about being older than me when we started dating, but I'm clearly the old one. He went out last night with friends on a Friday night; I was more than content to stay in on a Friday night and catch up on some sleep. The first night of our road trip, I asked Grant, "Can we please go to sleep soon?" at half past nine.

TUESDAY, MARCH 15, 2011

KFC is going to start selling a sandwich with chicken as the bun. It's all Bob and my coworkers are talking about today; they're all really excited to try it. Because I'm American, they think I eat American fast food, but I don't—I hate it. I hate McDonald's. I hate American pop music. I do not eat McDonald's or listen to pop music, but the rest of the world seems to equate me with these things because I'm American.

My country is inescapable. Even in Samoa, there were two McDonalds' and a Pizza Hut. There were only two radio stations on the island. Most of the music I heard coming from radios in cars and houses was American pop music. I would be woken up to crappy American pop music from the neighbors blasting their radio and roosters crowing.

THURSDAY, MARCH 17, 2011

Today was Grant's day off from work, and he spent it in the library, researching carnivorous plants. He explained, "A kid's TV show is coming into my work to film an episode about carnivorous plants. I don't know any of the native plants in New Zealand, so I have to study up."

"You're going to be on TV? What's the show called?"

"It sounds rather dubious, but it's a kid's show on Sticky TV. I have to talk about New Zealand's carnivorous plants on the show."

"Are they paying you?"

"No."

"Are you getting paid to do research on your day off?"

"No."

"I think your work and Sticky TV are exploiting you for your cool accent. They really should pay you."

112

FRIDAY, MARCH 18, 2011

A customer on the phone was upset that the next available inspection time wasn't until next Monday, so he said, "Please, can you help me? I want it sooner than that."

I said, "I'm trying to help you, but there are only so many hours in the day. If they're all booked, it's not like I can add more hours to the day."

There's a delay in inspection books because inspectors were sent to Christchurch to help with the earthquake. The inspectors have been coming back to work, looking traumatized and saying things like, "There is no water there; I couldn't shower the whole time I was there. I've never seen grown men cry before—or such denial. A man had a crack going down the center of his house. I told him it was unsafe to continue living there. He was in such shock and denial, all he kept saying was, 'But I just bought that house.'"

Some customers think having a few days of delay for their inspections is unacceptable, even after I explain that we sent inspectors to Christchurch. They're annoyed and say, "There isn't usually a three-day wait for inspections."

"There usually isn't a national disaster," I respond. "I'm sorry you think your problem is bigger than Christchurch."

I'm a smart ass, and I don't care. I don't get paid enough to care. Not the right attitude, but I don't care. I'm a temp. If I don't want to talk to someone or if they're yelling at me, I say sweetly, "Can you hold please?" and either hang

113

up or transfer their call to a random number or to the call center. When I'm really not in the mood, I just keep them on hold until they hang up. I find this method the most satisfying because no one else can call in with the annoying customer on hold.

SUNDAY, MARCH 20, 2011

I adore Grant. I only have one pillow that we share and snuggle all night. Sickeningly sweet, he doesn't mind sharing one pillow. At one point, his elbow was pressing down on the top of my head. When I tried to move his elbow, my ponytail was in the crook of his arm and was yanked with the movement of his arm. My friend Lily's response to this story was, "Puke."

TUESDAY, MARCH 22, 2011

There's a gold-package movie deal for a hundred dollars at the cinemas here. The hundred dollars gives you admission for two for a feature-length film and a bottle of wine. This seems like an outrageous price to me. I'm too cheap to enjoy this. I would be sitting in the dark, not paying attention to the screen and just calculating how many dollars per minute the movie was costing me. This country has legal prostitution. Prostitutes roam the streets not too far from the theater. I haven't inquired, but I would guess a blow job would be less than going to the movies. If the gold-package movie deal costs a hundred dollars, I would expect sexual services and a guaranteed orgasm or your money back.

WEDNESDAY, MARCH 23, 2011

The last customer I talked to asked if I was from the
Philippines. I started laughing so hard that I had to put
him on hold. I told him, "I'm from California but currently
in Auckland."

As far as I can tell, Council is primarily run by international
temps. This fact confuses customers when they call and
expect to hear a Kiwi accent.

THURSDAY, MARCH 24, 2011

I realized that I had reached my cubicle burnout point with
my job when I didn't want to hear one more customer
complaining that I couldn't book him an exact time for an
inspection, only morning or afternoon. A customer
complained about it being a stupid policy, and I snapped.

I ranted for about five minutes, saying, "I completely
agree, it is a stupid policy, but it is not my policy. This is
not my government, this isn't my country, I have
absolutely no authority here. I am a temp. I think the
policy is stupid too. It's having annoying conversations like
this with customers like you that makes my job so horrible.
Would you please write a letter to Council? Seriously,
would you like me to transfer you to someone with
authority? I'm sick of having conversations like this. All
day, every person I have to book an inspection for
complains about this. It's really annoying, and I don't see
why it can't be changed."

115

I realized that I was beginning to shout, and the cool-as-a-cucumber Irish temp Mark in the cubicle next to me was starting to look scared of me. He had stopped what he was working on and was looking at me like I was a lunatic. I looked around the cubicles; others were looking at me out of the corners of their eyes.

I stopped my cubicle rage rant. I was starting to scare myself. I was screaming at a complete stranger on the phone, telling him, "It is people like you, sir, that ruin my day." I cleared my throat. The man at the other end was too frightened to speak. I sighed and said calmly, "Well, umm…so I have you booked for next Tuesday in the afternoon."

"OK. Thanks." The man sounded startled. A little girlie-sounding California voice had ripped him a new one.

I tried to sound calm and less insane, "So would you like to be transferred to the team leader to talk about the policy?"

"No, thanks. Have a good day," he said quietly and hung up.

FRIDAY, MARCH 25, 2011

After having a huge fight with Bob, the psychotic mime, about Aborigines and Native Americans, I stood up and screamed, "You're a dick!" so loudly that all the heads popped over the cubical walls like meerkats on the prairie. They all had wide eyes and stared at me as I screamed at

116

him and ran off crying.

I used the customer bathroom to sob in because it's a single stall, and I wanted privacy. There was a line of about five guys waiting to use the bathroom. I cut in front of them all, locked the door, and cried loudly about the injustices of indigenous people during colonization and since then. I cried because these problems were widespread across the world, irreversible, and I couldn't figure out any way to help. After about fifteen minutes, I managed to compose myself. I emerged from the bathroom with red, puffy eyes to see five guys who looked like they were about to pee their pants.

I e-mailed my temp agency to see if there were any other positions available. My temp agent called to tell me there were no other jobs for me and to see what my problem was. I carefully said, "It's not the job, it is the person sitting next to me. I don't know where to begin explaining or where to end. His behavior has been less than professional."

"Oh, I know exactly who you're talking about," she explained without me saying a name. "We've received several complaints about him by several people, but we have no other temp jobs available for your skill set."

I thought, "Then why the fuck am I sitting next to him? What does a person need to do to get fired in this country?"

It turns out that every single girl in the office has had a problem with him, and he tortured all the temps before me. I decided it has to end with me. I don't get paid enough to deal with this shit. The job is crappy enough as is. I'm already telling customers on the phone that their conversations make my job so horrible. I don't need to be sitting next to a sexist, racist, bloodsucking, perverted mime.

I don't want to do this anymore. My cubicle is killing my soul. I want to do something that matters, something that has a positive impact on the world. I want to be creative. I don't want to be a tool in a system. I don't want to be a monkey running on a barrel. Everyone around me seems perfectly content to be sitting in their gray cubicle in their gray clothes. I'm not.

SATURDAY, MARCH 26, 2011

My little old neighbor Jim had an art show that I brought Grant to. I told Grant, "Jim's my older neighbor friend," as we walked to his show.

"What do you consider old?" Grant asked, still feeling insecure about the age gap.

"Well, Jim's a grandpa."

I introduced Grant to Jim, who smiled and told Grant, "You're being looked after by an angel."

After the show we walked through a park. I asked Grant, "What were you doing when you were twenty-seven?"

He stopped, "Do you really want to know?"

"Yes."

"I was preparing to get married. We were too young, and I felt pressured into it. It didn't last. I'm divorced now."

"I know. It's OK, I could be divorced now too. I was engaged when I was too young too, but I broke off the engagement. I felt like I was already in a middle-aged, sexless marriage and didn't want to go through with the wedding. Do you have any kids?"

"No, thank goodness."

SUNDAY, MARCH 27, 2011

I want to move out of my cottage. I'm over the bugs, being cold, and not being able to cook. Bob the mime was looking at my cottage on Google maps and said he's going to tap on my windows in the middle of the night.
I'm very overwhelmed. I agreed to pay one-third of the total electric bill shared with the main house that my little one-room cottage is behind. After I was shocked by my one-third coming to ninety dollars a month for my one lightbulb, I asked my landlord to come up with a new solution or get a meter. She told me a meter costs $1,500 to $3,000 to install. My landlord said sort it out with the front house or move out. Apparently, I'm the first person in ten years to have an issue with paying one-third of the bill.

It's embarrassing having friends over because they're immediately swarmed by mosquitoes. The amount of bugs in my house makes me feel like I'm camping. I'm not even killing them because I've given up. Moths and larva are covering my kitchen, and all my food is ruined. There are cockroaches everywhere, and all sorts of spiders.

Yesterday, I saw something that looked half-scorpion, half-spider next to my towel when I got out of the shower. There was a praying mantis above my bed. I'm constantly swarmed by mosquitoes and woken up every single night when bitten. I'm completely covered in mosquito bites from head to toe. Citronella candles and bug repellant don't work. Now that it's becoming autumn, it's hard to sleep because I'm so cold.

It takes me forty-five minutes to walk to work and even more time by bus because there is no route to my work.

I'm over all of the above.

To complicate things, Grant found out that the owner of his house is coming back to the house, and everyone needs to be out in seven weeks. I like living alone but spend most of my alone time screaming at and squishing bugs. I chase them around my cottage, clapping at the air and slapping my body. I'm constantly covered in itchy bites.

I'm going back to the United States for three weeks in April. Grant's giving me a ride to the airport. If I need to move, I need to move now or put all my stuff at Grant's, and then figure it out in May and save money on rent for the three weeks I'm in California.

I have very little money because I live paycheck to paycheck and am paying all of these extra, unexpected bills. Council has free milk for employees to put in their coffee. I've been bringing cereal into work and using the Council's milk, eating two or three bowls of cereal a day, just to avoid spending money on food.

This week I have a job interview to be a venue reservation coordinator for Council on Thursday. Tomorrow I have a meeting with HR to take down Bob the mime—three other girls in the office and I are making a formal complaint.

MONDAY, MARCH 28, 2011

A giant moth the size of a butterfly just flew out of my purse at work. I unknowingly brought it to my cubicle from my Amazon jungle–like Grey Lynn cottage. It's now flying around the cubicles in my office and terrifying people.

TUESDAY, MARCH 29, 2011

Today the crazed mime Bob is off work, and all the managers are at off-site training. I'm being an extra sassy smart ass on the phone with customers. I'm so sarcastic and sassy that I'm making them laugh. My phone cord was so tangled I couldn't lift the phone up, so I switched it with Bob's perfectly untangled cord. He will probably switch it back, but the satisfaction I already have that he will be so outraged that I fucked with his OCD sanitized desk is making me smile all day.

WEDNESDAY, MARCH 30, 2011

I've heard that only two hours of work gets done a day in offices. Temps do more, fearing they won't get future jobs. The permanent staff members work less, giving the temps their work to do. The longer the permanent staff members have been working at Council, the less work they do. At this office, I've seen many things that are not work being done by the permanent staff.

I've heard from a Kiwi that Council is known for being run by slackers. I'm not a slacker, per se, it's just that the work that I'm doing is not my job. I spend the majority of my workday typing up all crazy shit that happens in cubicles—as long as you keep typing, no one questions what you're typing.

THURSDAY, MARCH 31, 2011

I'm a candidate to be a venue reservation coordinator at Council. I thought my interview was at eleven in the morning on Thursday. Turns out that it was at eleven on Wednesday. I got a phone call at noon, asking, "Where are you? You had an interview today and didn't show."

Surprise! I can't read a calendar. This seems like an essential skill for a venue reservation coordinator. Want to hire me to book other people's reservations when I can't figure out what day to show up to the interview on? Yes, apparently Council does.

I even had a friend e-mailing, "Good luck with your

interview." Nothing clicked. I was confused about why she was e-mailing me good luck a day early. They rescheduled me to have my interview on Friday, April 1. I'm a fool with an interview on April Fools' Day. On the way to the interview, I e-mailed my current boss that I was leaving the office and going to a different Council building. If I get this position, I will have worked in all the Council buildings due to all of the temp jobs I've had.

My boss e-mailed me back, wishing me luck and saying, "I started out as a temp at Council with a two-week contract, and now I've been at Council for sixteen years."

Terror. Absolute terror fell over me. What if I'm in a black hole that I can't get out of at Council?

SATURDAY, APRIL 2, 2011

The Seasonal Monologues is Thomas Sainsbury's current show. He told me to watch it and observe the other performers because I'll be performing my monologue soon. I've watched it two nights in a row and just feel more confused and nervous. I'm not an actress. All of the performers in The Seasonal Monologues are real actors; one was even on a TV show.

At the beginning of the year, Tom met me about my monologue; his only instructions were, "Just write about your experiences in New Zealand." Tom patiently listened to my rough draft and laughed at my life. After my long story, Tom asked, "What is the point of this story, Jamie? How long is it? It only needs to be 1,500 words. And you realize you will have to perform this."

I shrugged and almost burst into tears. "I don't know what the point is. I've never done this before. I don't know what I'm doing. It's over 4,500 words. I sincerely don't understand how it's performing if it's me telling my story."

SUNDAY, APRIL 3, 2011

Grant took me to a beach called Whatipu—funny name but a really beautiful beach. We walked along the beach. It was gorgeous, but there were mirages in the sand that made it look like it just ended, like it was the edge of the world, in the distance. The strange thing about New Zealand is that the isolation feels palpable. It really feels like you're at the end of the world. We sat and looked out at the ocean. Grant asked if I wanted to live with him.

Everything is just simple with Grant, in the best sense of the word. It's just easy to be with him. He has never played any games with me; we have never needed to set any rules or have the talk about where this is going. We're both total dorks and make each other laugh all day.

It feels natural to move in with him. He's so kind, and respectful, and cute, and funny. I don't think I truly understood the word intimacy before I met him. He's very sensitive and looks so vulnerable and innocent. It was like we have a clean slate, the past is in the past. We left our emotional baggage in our countries in other hemispheres. Grant's so handsome but so humble. When I tell him he's handsome, he blushes and says, "You're very kind to me."

Even though he's older, I'm the one who needs to be gentle with him.

MONDAY, APRIL 4, 2011

Today I began training as a venue reservation coordinator and then was offered the job. Things seem to happen backward when you're on the bottom of the world. After I had my interview last week, they called my current boss and told her that they were impressed with me, despite the fact I couldn't read a calendar and missed my first scheduled interview. They arranged for me to look at the computer system they described as complex during an interview at half past nine today.

Today Bob had a meeting with HR, and I was afraid to be in that office. The new job appears to be easier than the job I was doing next to Bob the mime. I figured out the so-called complex system on the first try. They offered me the job and asked, "What do you expect to be paid? How much are you making now temping?"

"Not enough." This is where I fucked up. I should have asked for more money. "I don't want to get paid less than I'm making now."

TUESDAY, APRIL 5, 2011

I seem to have met the male version of me at Council. Andrew Mockler is the person I'm replacing as a venue reservation coordinator. My new boss, Selma Shark, went home sick after Andrew arrived two hours late. After training me on the complex computer system for fifteen minutes or so, we discovered we have similar slacking off skills. We went on YouTube, where he showed me songs he sang and wrote. Then I showed him the stories I've been writing on the clock.

He read a story last week about the interview on April Fools' Day. He laughed, "That was you that didn't show up to the interview? I told them they probably shouldn't hire you if you couldn't figure out what day the interview was."

He showed me all the songs he wrote in his cubicle, and I told him I wrote a novel on the clock. Then we added each other as friends on Facebook. In England, he used to be Sting's backup singer. I have no idea what he's been doing working for Council.

At lunch, I told him about Bob the psychotic mime in the cubicle next to me and how I don't want to go back to that cubicle even though my contract doesn't end for another two days. I threw the grenade to HR and ran. He told me, "Nothing crazy like that will happen in this job; you can do the week's worth of work Monday morning and just go online the rest of the week." He said he's been over an hour late every day for over a year. It's impossible to get fired. But I have to warn you, everyone in the office has filed formal complaints about one another. The ring leader is an angry, middle-aged woman on the other side of the cubicle wall, Judith. I've filed a formal complaint about Judith complaining too much about everyone else."

Council seems to have a surplus of angry, middle-aged women who glare at me. We got in trouble for laughing too much by the middle-aged Judith who shares the cubicle wall. Hope they open the male brothel soon. Not for me, but for all of the angry, middle-aged women who glare at me in the cubicles at Council. Judith stared at me for a long time, glaring at me while I smiled awkwardly at her, and then she looked down at my boobs and then glared at my face again.

Sitting on the other side of me is a girl named Gretchen who I caught spinning in circles with an air freshener in the bathroom. She puts deodorant on every fifteen minutes and wears her dead dog's collar around her neck. The dog died six months ago. She runs through the office like a panicked penguin. I applied for this same job seven months ago. They hired her instead of me.

THURSDAY, APRIL 7, 2011

The director, Thomas Sainsbury, and his producer came over to my cottage for a rehearsal of my monologue. I was beyond nervous. When I get nervous, I laugh. I was really nervous—ridiculously manic, hyperactive—I couldn't sit and pacing back and forth while laughing hysterically.

The only piece of furniture I have is a futon that Natalie gave me. Tom and the producer sat on the futon as I paced maniacally out of nervousness. Tom told me to sit on my suitcase that I store in my small kitchen. Shaking and perched on my suitcase, I read my story I had edited down to 1,500 words about a mime wanting to cut of my arm with a machete in a cubicle.

Tom said it was great and to memorize it and we will figure out things when I get back from California. The producer guy looked so scared of me, like he was thinking, "Forget switching to decaf; lay off the crack, crazy little American girl."

I almost started crying before he left. My nervous energy turned to terror. I'm going to have to figure out how to perform this.

FRIDAY, APRIL 8, 2011

When Grant has a drink, he raises his glass and says, "Chin, chin."

The other night, we were watching my new friend, the lost pop star Andrew Mockler, play a gig at a nearby bar with my friend Kana, who is Japanese. Grant and Kana had beers. Grant raised his glass to Kana, "Chin, chin."

Giggling, shaking her head and wagging her finger at him, Kana said, "Very naughty."

"Does that mean something other than "cheers" in Japanese?"

"Yes," Kana giggled. "Chin, chin means dick in Japanese."

SATURDAY, APRIL 9, 2011

Moving made me realize I've accumulated so many things that no longer fit in my one suitcase. I used plastic bags from grocery stores to pack the rest of my belongings. With a lack of packing materials, I tried to be creative, like wrapping clothes around dishes for padding.

I'm storing my things at Grant's place while I visit my family in California. He's living with flatmates now, but we'll get our own place when I get back. When it came time to move, Grant was so polite that he wouldn't let me carry or lift anything. He moved my suitcase and all of my random plastic bags into his car, drove the couple blocks to his house, unpacked, and came back to pick me up.

The first morning I woke up in his bed, I thought, "That was nice. I'm ready to go home now." Then I looked around the room, saw all of my belongings stuffed in plastic bags and remembered I lived with him now. I must have had a funny expression on my face. Grant looked at me and sweetly said, "Oh, you look like a wee trapped rabbit. I promise not to steal your independence."

SUNDAY, APRIL 10, 2011

Grant's flatmates are out of town, and I've been sitting in the empty house by myself. Grant met up with an old friend from Scotland who now lives in Palmerston North with his family. It was a guy's night out that I wasn't invited to. I wasn't expecting to meet his friend. Grant still needs to make a copy of his house key, and he left me in the house with his key. Around eight o'clock, I heard a knock at the door. It was Grant trying to get in.

All the doorknobs in New Zealand are different from other doorknobs. Most doors in New Zealand don't have knobs like in America but strange latches and locks that I can never figure out how to turn. Grant is always a gentleman and opening doors for me. I literally had never attempted to open his door from the inside before. Standing outside, he tried to talk me through opening the door. After about five minutes, I said, "I'm sorry, but I really can't figure this out. Why don't you just go around the back?"

Eventually I opened the door. To my mortification, Grant wasn't alone; his friend was standing behind him, looking at me with a concerned look in his eyes. Grant introduced us. His friend was over a foot taller than me, and we shook hands awkwardly. I wasn't expecting to meet anyone that evening, so I had my crazy curly hair in a tangled ponytail on top of my head and a purple plaid jacket with a fur trim. I hadn't attempted to unpack, and the room was lined with my random belongings in plastic bags.

Grant is older than me but looks young and innocent. His friend is the same age as Grant, mid-thirties, but has a wife and three kids. He has a look about him that tells you he's a father. Unlike Grant, the friend has the air of a proper adult.

Grant collected his house key from me, and they left to continue catching up over drinks. Grant returned a couple hours later, slightly intoxicated and giddy. "Sorry to leave

130

you alone. We hadn't seen each other for about five years and had a lot of catching up to do."

"Yeah, I guess you had to explain to your friend that you're now divorced, living in New Zealand, and keeping a young American hostage in your bedroom filled with plastic bags."

TUESDAY, APRIL, 12, 2011

Before visiting California, I've been craving American junk food. All I can think about is bacon, In-N-Out Burger, Ben and Jerry's, Red Vines, and Cheez-Its. My mom picked me up from the airport and drove me to In-N-Out. I was shocked by how loud America is. There's so much traffic, and everyone talks so loudly. I don't remember my mom talking so loudly before I left. I had to tell her to speak in a quieter voice because she was hurting my ears. Everyone in California seems to be moving too quickly. Everyone's rushing around, pushing, speaking loudly, and cell phones are ringing nonstop.

WEDNESDAY, APRIL 13, 2011

I was watching Power Rangers with my niece, and all the lines sounded familiar. Months back, I was running lines with my flatmate Liam, who was auditioning for the show that's filmed in New Zealand. I was trying to teach him how to speak in an American accent. My niece looked at me like I was a weirdo because I knew all the lines. Liam didn't end up getting the Power Rangers role. I could see him as a handsome leading heartthrob in a period piece more than a Power Ranger.

FRIDAY, APRIL 15, 2011

A wonderful thing that America does to its citizens is tax you on every dollar you earn, no matter what country you earn it in. It's called Universal Tax. I'm getting taxed twice for every dollar I make in New Zealand. Not only will I have to pay the New Zealand government tax, but I have to pay the US government tax on my New Zealand earnings. Exciting. No wonder there are so few of us working abroad.

While back in California visiting my family in April, I arrived just in time to pay taxes. In America, taxes are due April 15. My mom made me an appointment with H&R Block the day after I arrived. I showed up in the morning with my mom by my side and extremely jetlagged. I told the old lady at the front desk who seemed bewildered, as she didn't listen when I told her my name, that I had an appointment. She was flustered and confused with what I wanted and what I was doing there. I repeated my name several times, and then my mom repeated to her that we had an appointment.

"Oh, you should have told me you had an appointment," she huffed. "Take a seat. We'll be with you shortly."

My mom sat down, and I went to the cheap, but free, coffee station at reception. I needed more caffeine to deal with this. I slurped down a bitter cup with instant, dried

132

milk added. Cheap and dirty, but it did the trick. I was more alert when the second really old woman came to do my taxes.

My meager New Zealand earnings became even more miniscule when they were converted to US dollars that were then taxed. When my mom found out how little I earned last year, she looked alarmed, "How have you been living on that?"

The old lady doing my taxes seemed equally bewildered by my questions and her job. She slowly typed my info into the simplified system with one finger. I'm not patient and had to bite my tongue to not say, "Let me just type it! You're too slow!"

I told her my concern about being taxed twice. She said, "Well, you can get your double tax amended."

"Great, how?"

"I don't know, it's really complicated."

"Is there a website you can give me to do that?"

"I'm sure there is, I just don't know what it is."

At this point, I was frustrated because I'm being taxed twice; I'm shaking from too much coffee; and fighting off tears of frustration while trying to keep my eyes open. This old lady is being completely useless and charging $140 for her lack of service.

Behind me another old lady is helping someone else at a different desk and having trouble with her computer. She was calling the computer a "machine." She asked a feeble front-desk receptionist for help, who responded, "If you right click, the machine does different things."

SATURDAY, APRIL 16, 2011

It's fun to play the role of irresponsible aunt. When my seven-year-old niece told me a kid at school was beating her up, I said, "He sounds like a jerk, do you want me to come to your school and kick him in the butt?" At least I didn't say "ass."

My niece said, "Auntie Jamie, violence is never the answer."

At the park I pushed my niece on the swing really high, and she would jump off to see how far she could be launched. We did that most of the day. The rest of the kids at the park wanted me to push them too. I'm sure the park parents appreciated me creating a contest among the small children who launched themselves across the sand. My mom came to the park later and screamed with terror as she saw my niece fly through the air.

"She's fine. Don't worry, she won't hit the slide."

FRIDAY, APRIL 22, 2011

Yesterday I got the worst haircut ever. I went to my

grandma's hairdresser, an old lady with an old-lady fro. There were only other old ladies with their short hair in curlers who were wandering around the salon slowly, like zombies looking for live flesh to munch on.

I brought in a picture of Beyonce with long layers. My hair was mid back length, with ringlets at the bottom. The old lady cut my hair dry, grabbed the top third part of my hair and chopped it off a few inches from my scalp. I ended up with hair that looks straight but puffs out of the top of my head that goes higher than my ears, and the rest is long and curly, like Carol Brady with a curly mullet on the bottom.

The old lady who cut my hair gave up cutting and styling it. She tried washing it after she cut it, then she put a sticky product in it and tried to blow dry it. She didn't even know how to dry my hair; she had me lean upside down while she waved the blow dryer above my head. She had a small comb that got stuck in the long curls on the bottom half of my head.

When I raised my head back up, I had a puffy mushroom top with long dangling wet curls underneath. She said, "If your grandma wants her money back, that's fine."

She gave up even trying to fix my hair. Another lady tried to help her fix my hair but also failed. I walked out wide-eyed and with a dripping, mangled mullet. Everyone looked at me as I walked out.

I ran to my friend Grace's house after, and she was like, "What happened? Why do you have a mullet?"

135

I'm supposed to be performing a monologue in front of a live audience for the first time in my life next month, and the top layer is too short to fit into a ponytail. I went home with a straight bob on the top of my hair and long, stringy curls underneath running the length of my back. There is no way to blend the layers. It would grow back crazy. It's just a bit devastating to go in with an example picture of Beyonce's long layers and come out with a Carol Brady–type haircut. It's literally like Carol Brady, except my hair underneath is much longer, thinner, and curly. It's like bipolar hair. I tried to straighten it, but it looked stringy. I could try to keep it straight, but New Zealand is extremely humid. It's pointless for me to straighten it; when I try, it springs back curly.

I went to another place and asked them if they could fix it. They said, "Oh God, you got butchered. The only way I can transition the top layer is if I cut seven inches off the bottom. Unless you want to lose all of your length just put it in a ponytail for a few months."

It was that bad.

My options were to have a mullet or cutting nearly a foot off my hair. I now have hair above my shoulder.

SATURDAY, APRIL 23, 2011

I went to the mall with my best friend Grace, who lovingly refers to me as Little Miss Crazy Pants because of how I am. We went into H&M, and I ran around the shop, excited by all the sale racks. I held up a sweater marked down to one dollar and excitedly said to someone walking by me, "Oh my God, is this really only one dollar?"

The girl walking by stopped and looked me up and down like I was crazy. She said, "I don't know, I don't work here."

"Sorry, I'm just really excited."

After we left the store, I was sweating and out of breath. I panted to Grace as I fanned my face, "I'm sweating, are you sweating?"

"No, I'm not running around like a maniac. Simmer down, girl, you're acting crazy!"

We ended up having lunch at Applebee's. I hated Applebee's before I left California, but after a year in New Zealand, I was craving things New Zealand just didn't have, like buffalo wings, blue-cheese dressing, and mozzarella sticks. In the grocery stores in New Zealand, limes cost $29.99 per kilogram. There is only one Mexican restaurant in Auckland, the margaritas there sell for twenty dollars each. At Applebee's we ordered a pitcher of margaritas and a sampler platter for about seven bucks.

Over lunch, I told Grace strange temping tales. She said, "It sounds like weird shit is still happening to you, but you're dealing with it better."

"I guess it's the whole Buddhist thing—to not be swayed by your circumstances and be happy no matter what obstacles you face."

137

SUNDAY, APRIL 24, 2011

I hid eggs for my niece to find on Easter. Grant and I Skyped the other day, and he said, "Are you going to be rolling eggs on Easter?"

"What? We decorate them and then hide them and have Easter-egg hunts. Do you do that in Scotland?"

"No, as a kid, we would roll them down hills and chase them."

MONDAY, APRIL 25, 2011

In California I took advantage of free, women's-health clinics. I was nervous getting my yearly pap smear and exhausted from jetlag, so I had coffee before I went. I must have seemed a bit too over-caffeinated because the doctor examining me assured me that my lady parts were healthy; the only thing she was concerned about was my caffeine consumption. Instead of scolding me about safe sex, she said, "How many cups of coffee are you drinking a day?"

"Today I had two, but sometimes up to four or five because my job's really boring."

"Caffeine's a drug that we're all addicted to, but it's still a drug. You really need to be drinking more water."

138

SATURDAY, APRIL 30, 2011

Grant picked me up from the airport during the Royal Wedding weekend when Prince William and Kate were getting married. Grant casually said to me as he drove me around Auckland, "Are you planning to watch the Royal Wedding?"

I shrugged, oblivious to current affairs and popular culture. "Is that happening soon?"

"It's this weekend."

"Hmm."

"I don't want to sound anti-English, but I wasn't that impressed with Buckingham Palace when my dad got knighted," he said casually, as if everyone's dad was a knight.

"What? What are you talking about? Is your dad really a knight?"

"Yeah, it's not a big deal, they knight just about anyone these days."

"I'm pretty sure they don't just knight anyone. I honestly don't know much about the queen or the royal family or being a knight, but it kind of seems like a big deal."

We've been together for months and moved in together, and he's never mentioned it. He didn't seem like he wanted to talk about it, so I stopped prying. When I

Skyped with my dad next, I told him, "Grant's dad's a knight!"

There was a long pause, and then my dad excitedly said, "You mean like knight of the Round Table?"

"I guess so."

MONDAY, MAY 2, 2011

It's my first day back to work, and I get this e-mail:

Subject: Outcome of claims of Harassment

From: Ian Balless
Sent: Tuesday, 26 April 2011 12:25 p.m.
To: Jamie Baywood; Sarah Benmore, Jenny Simpson, Elizabeth Green
Subject: Outcome of claims of Harassment

PRIVATE AND CONFIDENTIAL

Hello Jamie, Sarah, Jenny, and Elizabeth,

This is to advise you of the outcome of the harassment claims that you raised.

I conducted an investigation into your claims of harassment and accepted that they had validity. However the evidence indicated that you didn't advise the harasser or anyone else of your discomfort

140

at the time of the harassment, and, therefore, it is reasonable to take the view that the harasser didn't realize the impact that he was having upon you.

I've discussed the case with the harasser's manager, and she's decided that there should be no formal disciplinary action taken against the harasser in this case. However, the harasser will have a letter placed on his file, which makes it clear that such behavior is inappropriate and which could be used as evidence of such advice should he engage in this type of behavior in the future.

May I also add that the harasser has assured me that he has learned a significant lesson from this and that he won't engage in this sort of activity in the future.

I hope that you find this outcome satisfactory.

There's no doubt that raising a matter such as this is a brave step, yet it's critical if harassment in the workplace is to be stopped. Many thanks for taking the initiative.

Regards,

Ian Balless

Senior HR Manager

Auckland

CAUTION: This e-mail memorandum and any attachments holds material that may be private and may be LAWFULLY CONFIDENTIAL. If you are not the planned recipient, any use, revelation, or replication of this memo or attachments is severely forbidden. If you have received this e-mail message in mistake, please inform us directly and remove all duplicates of the memo and attachments. We do not accept accountability for any viruses or alike passed with our e-mail or any properties our e-mail may have on the receiver computer or system. Any opinions conveyed in this e-mail may be those of the specific dispatcher and may not automatically replicate the opinions of Council.

WEDNESDAY, MAY 4, 2011

Gretchen, the girl wearing her dead dog's collar around her neck at my new job, got a phone call from a customer freaking out. They had a funeral booked at one of the venues, and their swipe card wasn't working. They had the casket at the door and couldn't get in. They screamed at Gretchen on the phone.

Selma Shark, the boss, is off sick. Gretchen went for a cigarette after the conversation. I looked worried, and Andrew told me, "Don't worry. That sort of thing happens all the time. The system doesn't work; it's really outdated and runs on a dial-up modem, but they're too cheap to fix it."

"Dial-up still exists?"

"It does in New Zealand."

142

SATURDAY, MAY 7, 2011

Grant and I found our own place, but we only have
enough furniture for the bedroom. New Zealand could use
an Ikea or Target. There are no furniture shops that we
could find anywhere in Auckland, the biggest city in New
Zealand. The thrift shops sell crappy old furniture for
hundreds of dollars. We are mystified by how people
we know have furnished homes, because we can't figure
out where the furniture comes from.

We drove around looking for furniture stores or charity
shops that sold furniture, but we couldn't find any. At one
point, we were stopped at a red light in front of a store
that only sold women's shoes in sizes ten and up.

I looked out the passenger-seat window, "Glad we found
the giant-women's shoe store. That's helpful and practical.
How do they stay in business? I haven't noticed Kiwi
women having really big feet. Do you think it's for the
cross-dressing men that work K' Road?"

"I don't know. Maybe we can buy a bunch of huge
women's shoes and construct our own couch, and table,
and chairs out of them."

I asked my friends where their furniture came from, and
they all said Trademe. I repeatedly asked my Kiwi friends,
"But where does it come from? I can't find stores that sell
furniture."

They would shrug and say, "Overseas?"

As far as I can tell, when foreigners moved to New Zealand, they would bring their own furniture and then sell it on Trademe when they moved away.

We sat on the ground and used cardboard boxes as tables. Grant, feeling homesick, said he wished our house had a hallway at the entrance because that's how houses are in Scotland. I made a hallway from cardboard as a joke.

Grant Skypes with his family once a week. The first time I Skyped with Grant and his family, we sat in front of our mock cardboard hallway and propped the laptop on our table, aka cardboard box.

This was the first time Grant's brother, sister-in-law, nephew, and parents saw me. After the introductions, Grant's older brother, looking concerned for his younger brother on a supposed adventure in New Zealand, said, "Grant, where are you?"

"Umm, in my house."

I looked down at our small image in the corner of the computer screen; all you could see behind us was cardboard. We looked like our house was made out of cardboard. We looked like we were in some sort of a hostage situation on the Skype screen. Even Grant's newborn nephew looked at us confused.

"In your house? What's with all the cardboard?"

Not helping our cause or my first impression on my new family, I tried to explain, "Oh, the cardboard behind us is

144

just a joke. I made Grant a fake hallway out of cardboard."

Grant tried to explain further, "We can't find any furniture here, so we're using cardboard boxes as tables." He patted the cardboard box the computer was on, which caused the screen to shake.

SUNDAY, MAY 8, 2011

I need to learn how to cook. I've been on the single-girl-without-a-real-kitchen, non-cooking diet of cereal, yogurt, fruit, oatmeal, carrot sticks, and hummus.

My cottage kitchen in New Zealand had a sink, mini fridge, hot plate, and toaster oven. This was much more advanced than my kitchen in my cottage in California. Before I left for New Zealand, I lived in an even tinier cottage that was approximately ten feet by twelve feet and didn't even have a kitchen sink. There was a microwave and a mini fridge. I would borrow glasses from my mom's house and drink water from the sink in the bathroom. I had regretted getting rid of my childhood Easy-Bake Oven.

I was working at Health Nuts at the time, where my managers constantly claimed they paid me too much, even though I couldn't afford to shop there. I would go to my mom's or grandma's for hot meals. I just kept yogurt and fruit in my cottage.

Our first week of living together, I sent a panicked e-mail to Grace back home:

145

What is the Moroccan recipe you told me about? I'm making dinner for Grant tonight. Need to impress him. Made him a salami-and-cheese sandwich last night. I miss you my dear friend.

The response I got:

Moroccan Chicken Tajine

Ingredients:

8 skinless chicken thighs
1/4 cup honey
1 large onion, chopped
3 garlic cloves minced
3 cinnamon sticks, 3 inches each
1 lemon, juiced
2 teaspoons turmeric
1 tablespoon of grated ginger
1/2 cup dried apricots, quartered
1 cup of chopped veggies (add in last 20 minutes)

What to do:

Put in chicken
Sprinkle on turmeric
Pour on honey
Sprinkle onion, garlic, apricots, and cinnamon sticks
Pour on lemon
Bake @ 300 degrees F (150 C) for 1 hour and 20 minutes in a covered pot

I miss you too! Have fun cooking this dish. You

know if you do, he will fall in love with you forever.
It's that powerful and beautiful too.

Love,
Grace

The meal was the most delicious thing I had ever made.

MONDAY, MAY 9, 2011

Gretchen is telling customers on the phone that her name
is, "Gretchen with a G, as in goat."

All day long, I'm hearing next to me, "Gretchen with a G,
as in goat."

TUESDAY, MAY 10, 2011

Thomas Sainsbury had me memorize my monologue and
recite it to him. I think I over-memorized it and sounded
stiff. He told me, "Pretend like I'm a friend and you're
telling the story for the first time."

That didn't seem to help my lack of performance. As I
recited the monologue, he threw a beach ball at me to get
me to relax and loosen up.

WEDNESDAY, MAY 11, 2011

Everyone called in sick today except me. The rest of the

teams on the floor are doing off-site training, so the entire floor is empty. Jim called late this morning. I answered since I was alone. I haven't had a chance to visit him since I've been back from California. He said, "I have terminal liver cancer. The doctors have given me six months."

"What?" I started crying on the phone.

"Don't worry, since it's in my liver, I'm not in pain. Can you come over and chant with me around noon?"

"I can't today. I've just started this new job, and no one is here; I'm the only one on the floor. Could I come by after work?"

"I've been really tired; I'm usually sleeping around then. Earlier in the day is better for me."

"OK, let's get together soon. Please keep in touch."

"I will, don't worry. I'm excited to see what happens next. I'm not scared. It will be an adventure."

THURSDAY, MAY 12, 2011

Early today, Gretchen said, "I don't drink or do drugs; I'm high on life every day."

She was hobbling around the office. I asked her, "What's wrong with you?"

"I was in a bad accident when I was a kid, and it affected my pelvis. That's why I walk like a duck. I took four tramadol today, but I'm still in pain."

She's not high on life, she's high on the opioid-based prescriptions that she pops like candy.

I had menstrual cramps and asked Andrew (the guy training me/lost pop star) for some aspirin. He gave me something that he said he got over the counter. I didn't realize it was a muscle relaxant. I was silent and nearly drooling the rest of the afternoon.

FRIDAY, MAY 13, 2011

This morning I received a phone call from a woman running a day care at one of the venues. There's a homeless man who sleeps on the back deck. He pooped on the back deck of the venue this morning, leaving the little kiddies a big surprise. Apparently he shits on the deck every day. I had to put an emergency work order in for poop cleanup. I wonder who had to clean the poop today.

This job is crappy, but at least I didn't have to clean up someone else's poop at work today.

SATURDAY, MAY 24, 2011

I went to see Kevin the Musical starring Steve Wrigley and Cyan, his fiancée and my friend. They are the funniest, most creative, and kindest couple I have ever met. Their show was absolutely hilarious. I love them both.

149

SUNDAY, MAY 25, 2011

Living with Grant is great, but we're still struggling to understand each other's accents. We have made a rule to not talk to each other unless we're facing each other in the same room. If one of us talks to the other from another room or if we aren't face to face, we can't understand each other.

I asked Grant if houses in Scotland had garbage disposals, like in America. He said, "No, but I read a book about a man that married an American woman, and he moved to America and describes them in his book."

THURSDAY, MAY 26, 2011

I've felt like a secret agent all week, working in the cubicle during the day and performing my monologue at night. I ended up writing a monologue about my temp jobs. I just told the truth; I said all the things you want to say at a job interview but never say.

Wednesday was the opening night. I had a panic attack before the first show, but the adrenaline rush of being on stage and making people laugh was the most amazing thing. Writing seems like a more honest form of creativity. With my painting, the best response I can get is, "That's interesting." With writing, people either laugh or they don't.

Grant's been in the audience every night. He's seen the show so many times that, when we get home, he recites lines from other performers' monologues. Thomas Sainsbury told me, "Blondie's in the front row is all smiles for you."

Every night, one of the real actors, Jane, has been telling me backstage superstitions. There's opening-night jitters, when the performances have lots of energy. The second night, the performers feel more confident and lose the energy from the opening night. Second-night audiences are never as great. The final night is always amazing but never the best performance.

After the shows, we've been talking to people in the audience. Everyone I've talked to asked me how long I've been acting. I told them, "I'm not an actress."

Rolling their eyes and thinking I'm being pretentious, they then ask, "How long have you been performing?"

"This is the first time I've done anything like this. Those are my real jobs; I have to work next to the girl wearing her dead dog's collar around her neck tomorrow."

Liam, my old flatmate, was also very supportive and came to watch the show. When people didn't believe my monologue, Liam said, "It's true. I used to live with her, and she would come home and tell me about her crazy days."

FRIDAY, MAY 27, 2011

Grant was laughing at me this morning, "You look like you've just been born when you wake up."

"What do you mean?"

"Like how baby cows are born and just start walking around."

I put my alarm clock across the room to force myself to get out of bed. Yesterday I got out of bed, hit snooze, fell on top of Grant, and then crawled under the fitted top sheet getting back into bed.

He laughed, "Are you going to sleep under there now?"

Grant had the day off of work, and I must have been hitting the snooze button too much. Grant pulled the covers off of me and gave me a gentle shove off the bed. "Off you go," and then he rolled over with his back to me with all of the covers.

SATURDAY, MAY 28, 2011

Grant's parents came to New Zealand to visit. I instantly loved them when they opened the door to their hotel room. They both gave me hugs and said it was great to see me in person instead of in pixels on Skype.

I asked his dad to tell me about being knighted.

"Oh, you know, I just knelt down, and the queen tapped her wee sword on my shoulder and just talked to me for a bit. It was a pretty brief process."

We went out to dinner, and my wine glass was constantly

topped up the entire evening. When Grant and I got back to our house, I thought it would be a good idea to drink the whiskey that his parents brought him from Scotland.

Needless to say, I was very hungover at work the next day. Grant told his parents I didn't have a Scottish tolerance. After learning about my low tolerance, they would ask, "Would you like just a wee glass of wine? Just a wee one?"

Grant has the same big blue eyes as his dad who told me, "It's hard for me to remember that wine is alcohol; to me it's like juice, it's like having one of your 5 A Days."

SUNDAY, MAY 29, 2011

Grant's parents brought him a suitcase of clothes. As his mom handed him the suitcase, she scolded him, "I can't believe you lost all your good clothes on the bus."

"You did?" I asked Grant.

I had wondered why he dressed in strange clothes that didn't fit him and his shoes were duct taped and stapled together.

"Aye, I had two bags of clothes. One bag of nice clothes and one bag of old gardening clothes. I accidently lost the bag of nice clothes on the bus. I went to buy a pair of trousers at a shop on Queen Street. I was told at the shop that men's trousers only come in one length in New Zealand. There aren't enough men to make trousers in different lengths. The jeans I got aren't long enough for

153

my legs."

He opened the suitcase and put on a black button-up jacket. I said, "You look like a prince in that. You're so handsome!"

MONDAY, MAY 30, 2011

Grant looks very Scottish. He's the palest and blondest man I've ever seen. If we were to ever have a baby, we wouldn't need an ultrasound to see the baby in the womb because it would glow in the dark, we're both so pale. We're too pale to procreate in New Zealand, where there's a hole in the ozone.

One of Grant's friends told his parents, "Grant's so pale we call him Albino G."

"Really? He's the one that keeps the best tan in the family."

TUESDAY, MAY 31, 2011

My favorite thing about Grant's parents coming to visit was hearing stories about Grant as a little boy. After telling his parents that I loved runt animals when I was a kid, his mom said, "That's probably why you ended up with Grant. He was always smaller than the rest of the kids; his legs were too long for his body until he was about twelve. He was small, but he could run fast."

Grant's the youngest in the family, and when he was old

enough to be left home alone, he would break things and tell his parents, "It was nae me, it was the cat."

When Grant was about eighteen months old and just learning how to walk, they went on a holiday to their family farm in the Highlands of Scotland. Grant's blond hair stuck straight up when he was that age, and they dressed him in bright-red overalls. There was a rooster on the farm that was at eye level with Grant. His dad said, "The cockerel must have seen him as a rival and knocked him to the ground and began pecking at him."

To this day, his older brother loves to say, "Grant was knocked over by a giant cock."

SATURDAY, JUNE 4, 2011

While Grant was hard at work, I took his parents to Waiheke Island to go wine tasting. There was a rainstorm blowing through that made sightseeing impossible, so drinking wine was the best way to stay warm on the wet and windy day.

The ferry-boat ride is about thirty minutes from Auckland to Waiheke. The ferry stopped off at the North Shore. Among the passengers picked up at the North Shore, there was a group of a half-dozen guys in wet suits carrying one paddle each.

One of these wet suit fellows waltzed up and down the

aisle while staring at me. I could feel him looking at me as he paced back and forth with the paddle. Grant's parents noticed the wet-suited man staring at me, and we began to wonder what he was doing on the boat.

The wet-suited man asked if he could sit with us. He sat across the table from me and looked intensely at me with dark, smoldering eyes. His dark hair was beginning to gray on the sides. His skin was tanned and weathered from years of surfing in the sun. His wide shoulders overflowed into the aisle as he stretched his long arms across the table. His giant clasped hands were inches away from mine. He continued to look at me intensely. I was worried he was going to ask me out or say something embarrassing to me in front of Grant's parents. I could tell he had a tale to tell, and he wanted me to hear it.

I looked over at Grant's parents, losing the staring contest with the strange man. His parents politely made conversation with the man as they looked at me like, "You make interesting friends, don't you?" The man told us his name was Simon. Simon and a group of men were paddling back to Auckland on stand-up paddleboards.

He said, "It takes two to three hours, but you could do it," while looking at me. Simon told us his tale, acting as if he was about to jump out of a helicopter into a war zone. He looked out the rain-streaked windows at the choppy water as the ferry boat bounced up and down. "My wife asked me, why do you have to do this today? Because I can do it, that's why. I told my two young daughters, 'You make sure to clean your rooms today and take care of your mum. Make her lunch today, and bring it to her in bed.' My wife just had surgery and can't get out of bed."

I was beginning to get less and less impressed. I would be so annoyed if I were bedridden and my husband wanted to ditch me with the kids all day when I couldn't get out of bed.

Simon continued his wannabe heroic tale, "I have GPS on my watch, so I know which way to go. I have a waterproof phone in my sleeve and can dial 555 to call the coast guard. I didn't bring a knife to stab sharks with because that would be testing fate." He looked at me for a reaction.

"There are only hammerhead sharks around here, though, right? They don't attack people," I said in a smart-ass tone.

"You're right, the last time someone was bitten was in 1976."

"I went boogie boarding at Stinson Beach in October, when it was breeding season for great whites in Northern California. There's lots of warning signs at the beach, and my friend that I went with said, 'Don't worry, if you get bitten, I'll yank you out of the water. A girl I know was bitten, and everyone got her out before she was eaten.'"

WEDNESDAY, JUNE 8, 2011

In New Zealand, you get the queen's birthday off for a long weekend. I asked my coworker Gretchen how her long weekend was, and she said, "I took care of a dog in heat all weekend."

"What? Why?" I asked.

"My flatmate was out of town, and his dog was in heat. We had to lock her in the bathroom. It got messy and smelly. But we couldn't leave her in the backyard or else all the dogs around the neighborhood would jump the fence and jump on her."

THURSDAY, JUNE 9, 2011

Jim died. I never got to see him alive again. Vicky and I went over to his house to see his body. He was placed in an open casket on the ground. The room was completely filled with white lilies that gave off a strong, sweet scent. I've never seen a dead body before. It wasn't scary; he just wasn't in there anymore. Vicky and I chanted Nam Myoho Renge Kyo three times, one last time with Jim, and cried and held each other.

The funeral called a tangi was amazing, a real celebration of his life. The marae was filled with hundreds of people— so many people that there weren't enough seats for everyone, and some people couldn't get inside. Jim had asked for chanting as his casket was brought in and when it left the building. There was traditional wailing and dance performances. In one of the performances, a man with a machete chopped up bouquets.

We were listed on the program as Japanese Buddhist chanters. It was funny because it's a Japanese form of Buddhism, but it was me and a handful of Kiwis chanting. I wonder if people were expecting monks in robes.

158

The speeches were amazing. Jim lived such a full life; he had been everywhere and done so many things. People talked about him visiting Africa and meeting Yoko Ono in New York. He was an amazing father, grandfather, husband, friend, artist, and person.

FRIDAY, JUNE 10, 2011

Since I started my new job a couple of months ago, my boss Selma Shark has never worked a full week. She's always off sick; she works a maximum of three days a week and leaves by three o'clock or earlier on most days. Selma screams really loudly at Gretchen and has started screaming at me too.

Another temp was hired, a nice Irish girl named Susie. Although Susie has been working here over a month, she hasn't been trained to do anything yet. Selma says she's too busy to train her. Susie has a desk in the corner and a computer hooked up to the Internet but has no phone line to answer the customer calls.

TUESDAY, JUNE 14, 2011

I'm getting really burned out. My visa only allows me to work temporary positions. I've heard most of the other people from different countries, like England, are allowed to work permanent jobs and are getting paid ten dollars an hour more than me.

My niece was crying on Skype over the weekend, asking,

159

"Why are you living in New Zealand?"

I had no good answer to give her. I've hated all my jobs.
None have had anything to do with anything I have
studied or am remotely interested in. I had never been in a
cubicle or office before New Zealand, and I hope to never
be in one again. I performed a monologue based on my
job experiences in The Foreign Monologues, and no one
believed my story was true.

The only reason I'm still here is Grant. New Zealand is the
only country in the entire world where we can both get
work visas. It's fucked up. We're both only allowed to visit
each other's countries for ninety days without working.

It's the best relationship I've been in; he's the sweetest
man I have ever met. We want to stay together
somewhere, but I can't go to his country to work, and he
can't go to mine. We both hate our crappy jobs in New
Zealand and want to leave but don't know where to go or
how. We want to have jobs that creatively challenge us, not
challenge our sanity. We are both burned out and want out
of New Zealand.

As a US citizen, I'm not allowed to work anywhere in the
world other than the United States, New Zealand, and
Australia. As a Scottish man over thirty, he's only allowed
to work in the United Kingdom, Europe, and New
Zealand. I feel blessed to have met him. I love him so
much. Everything is just easy and effortless with him—
other than where we can both live and work. We're trying
to figure out how and where our next step is.

SATURDAY, JUNE 18, 2011

We're going to have to move again. The place Grant and I moved into is literally falling apart. We moved into a house in Grey Lynn. It looked cute, with a Paris-decoration theme at the open house. It had high ceilings, huge windows, and tons of natural light. Grant wasn't available during the open house, and I was confused when he said the walls needed to be repainted and that it looked dingy when he picked up the keys.

The lady living here before us was dying of cancer and left to live with her children. She had smoked inside for over seven years; they baked cookies during the viewing to mask the smell. There were black smoke stains on the ceiling and black outlines from where all the pictures on the walls had been. Needless to say, the house reeked of cigarettes. It had many nails, hooks, and holes in the walls. There were also posters glued to the walls in the kitchen and black silhouette stickers stuck to all of the walls with images of Europe.

All the paint along the window seals was chipped and peeling off. The shower basin was black. The house was basically filthy when we moved in and essentially imploded after we unpacked.

On our first night, we scrubbed the house for hours before we unpacked. In the morning, Grant turned on the stove to boil water for tea. When he turned the switch, the knob fell off, there was a loud popping sound of the coil exploding, and the power went out.

A couple weeks later, the blinds in the bedroom on the window facing the street fell off completely. We put a sheet up for privacy. Then the kitchen sink detached itself from the bench top, sinking a few inches below the bench top. We washed our dishes in the bathroom and patiently waited for the landlady to make the necessary repairs to the house, but they haven't been fixed.

One day, I discovered the bedroom walls, bedroom furniture, clothes, and some shoes were covered in green mold. None of the houses where I have lived in New Zealand have been insulated. It's normal to see your breath inside, large amounts of condensation on windows, and everything feeling damp and smelling musty.

Our neighbor is a stumbling but friendly drunk who brews his own beer under the house. We moved out as quickly as possible after I wrote a letter to the landlady.

Here's the e-mail I sent her:

From: Jamie Baywood
Date: Sat, Jun 18, 2011 at 11:56 AM
Subject: notice

Dear Rochelle,

Thank you for the opportunity to live in your rental. Due to the unforeseen essential repairs that were not apparent during the open house, we have found a new place to live. We completely understand that these repairs take time, we have been trying to be patient, but most of these problems have not been fixed since we moved in about a month ago.

We are grateful that the stove and the electrical outage have been repaired. But as you know, the sink had separated from the bench top the first week we moved in, and just the other day the hot-water knob on the kitchen sink completely fell off. We no longer have hot water in the kitchen and are having to bring hot water from the bathroom to do our dishes.

The blinds in the bedroom on the window facing the street completely fell off a couple weeks ago. We have been using a sheet for privacy ever since. The window-treatment company came to do measurements of the windows over a week ago, but they told us nothing could be done until the new coverings have been paid for. We gave them your contact information for invoices but have not heard anything more since the windows have been measured.

We have been informed that the painter, the new kitchen, and the insulation are lined up at the end of the month. Although the house is lovely and has potential to be a wonderful home, it currently is uninhabitable due to all of the renovations that need to take place. Realistically these repairs should be done before renting the house out because it is becoming increasingly difficult to live here.

We have the opportunity to move into a place that is

ready to live in next weekend, Saturday, June 25. It is our understanding that the painter is scheduled to begin sanding down and repainting the house next week as well, and due to the fact the previous tenant smoked inside for seven years, the painting job will take over a week.

We understand that we signed a contact stating that we are required to give twenty-one days' notice in writing, but we were hoping to come up with a solution that would be mutually beneficial. We were hoping that we could move out next week. As you stated yourself, Rochelle, it would be easier to do all of the reconstruction and repairs without people living in the house. The sooner we are able to leave, the sooner the house can be repaired and be rented out again.

Perhaps with all of the repairs, you will be able to charge a higher rent, possibly even taking advantage of the Rugby World Cup coming up. I am sure once the repairs are done you will have no problems instantly renting out the house—it does have the potential to be lovely and is in an ideal location.

We understand your situation, you have to work around several companies' schedules to coordinate the necessary repairs, and these things take time. We have no resentment; we just simply want to get out of the way for you to make these repairs possible.

Please understand that it was not our intention to rent

on such a short-term basis. Neither of us has ever asked to be released from a lease early. We just simply want to be able to have a home that is ready to live in now and have the opportunity to do so next week.

Please just let us know how to proceed from here. We have paid a bond of $975 and paid two weeks rent in advance when we moved in.

Kind Regards and Best Wishes,

Jamie and Grant

TUESDAY, JUNE, 21, 2011

Grant and I went to The Classic Comedy Bar to watch Steve Wrigley perform. I'm so lucky to have met all of these people to entertain me.

FRIDAY, JUNE 24, 2011

Tom directed another set of monologues, and this week we watched the Maori Monologues.

SATURDAY, JUNE 25, 2011

We moved into a spilt-level villa in Herne Bay, just a couple of blocks away from the beach. The living room has an enormous, elaborately carved mantel for the fireplace, with cathedral-like seats on either end. The mantel takes up almost the entire wall. Grant says it looks like we could go to Narnia through it. This place is special; it seems like it would have secret passages or something.

TUESDAY, JUNE 28, 2011

Susie the Irish temp requested that Matador Temp Agency reassign her to a different job since she still hasn't been trained. Selma Shark has been coming into work more often—some weeks she even works four days in a row. As part of our training, we took a tour of the venues that we book.

Selma is friends with an Australian lady named Tammy, who has long frizzy black hair, is covered in tattoos, is almost as wide as she is tall, and works in the office. Tammy speaks very loudly in a husky voice. Her cell-phone ringtone is set to the Queen song "Bohemian Rhapsody." It rings throughout the day, and you can hear it and her speaking loudly on it throughout the floor all day long.

Tammy drove us around Auckland and had major road rage. Tammy said to Selma, "I'm not going to say anything racist, but just look at the car in front of us. He's wearing a turban."

Selma was in the passenger seat and said, "Hey, some of us are PC in this car," glancing back at me sandwiched between Gretchen and Susie and awkwardly smiling like, "Are we really working right now? Or is this some sort of international temp-hostage situation?"

Selma elbowed Tammy, "Don't make fun of nappy head," and they both cackled.

The venues we viewed looked like small sheds or insane asylums. Most had such sticky floors that I found it difficult to lift my feet, garbage in piles outside, tire tracks in the grass, and a general stench. Some had balloons in the chandeliers and puke in the sinks. I can't believe people have their weddings in these venues.

WEDNESDAY, JUNE 29, 2011

Gretchen received a call from the call center about a person trapped in a venue on Waiheke Island. The person trapped in the venue wasn't even booked for that day. No one knows how they got in, and they couldn't figure out how to get out.

THURSDAY, JUNE 30, 2011

Gretchen changed the ringtone for the Venue Reservations on-call, after-hours phone to The Muppet's "Mahna Mahna" song because she likes it. It seems appropriate. Council is run by Muppets and international temps.

FRIDAY, JULY 1, 2011

I just overheard Tammy complain that the work car she had to use yesterday "reeked of marijuana, and it must

167

have been because it was parked next to a Chinese person or something."

This lady has a grandson on the way; her son knocked up a nineteen-year-old. They have plans to pierce her fetus grandson's ears and put him in a leather jacket when he's out of the womb.

MONDAY, JULY 4, 2011

Over the weekend, the office was robbed. Tammy happened to be in the building photocopying flyers for her cat-rescue event at three in the morning. Guess what, Tammy is a crazy cat lady too. She has hundreds of abandoned cats at her house.

When I got into work this morning, Tammy went around the office with a notepad, nervously helping make a list of stolen items. She asked me if anything was stolen at my desk. I opened my drawer, "Nope, I just keep tampons and snacks at my desk. I guess the robber didn't want to steal those."

Computers and other electronic equipment were stolen, and Judith, the office bitch, had her iPod taken. Our office is on the seventh floor, and the only way to get up in the elevators is with a swipe card that only employees have. I'm not a detective, but as soon as Tammy came around with her notepad, it was obvious that it was her.

Poor Susie was interrogated by the head-office managers for hours.

TUESDAY, JULY 5, 2011

It's my understanding that prostitutes have to detach themselves emotionally during their jobs. I realized that that is exactly what I have been doing in a cubicle for a year now. I have become numb to the meaninglessness of my work, the angry customers yelling at me, and the psychos I sit next to.

Susie said, "This job is soul crushing. It's getting harder and harder to come to work every day. I feel really depressed since I started this job."

I tried to comfort her by saying, "I've been temping for Council for a year now. This job sucks, but it's not the worst I have had, and it pays better than the other jobs that I've had. At my last job, the guy that sat to me text messaged pictures of his dick to girls in the office and told me he wanted to cut off my arm with a machete to drink my blood. When I told the temp agency, they were like, 'Sorry, we don't have any other jobs right now.' I approached HR with three other girls and presented all of our evidence. HR did absolutely nothing."

Susie's complained to Matador Temp Agency that she hasn't been trained, and I've complained that Gretchen and I are getting screamed at. They've just told us, "There are no other jobs available."

Welcome to temping at Council.

WEDNESDAY, JULY 6, 2011

Judith asked me if I liked my job.

I'm a smart ass and responded, "I'm living the dream one cubicle at a time. I got a tattoo that says, 'I Heart Council,' but since they changed the logo, I had to get it fixed by my tattoo artist."

Blank stares were my only response.

THURSDAY, JULY 7, 2011

We watched The Family Wilder, a play by Thomas Sainsbury, after work today. At work, the system crashed. Selma was away sick, so it was just Gretchen and me answering the angry phone calls and hundreds and hundreds of angry e-mails. I'm so grateful I have plays I can escape to after work.

FRIDAY, JULY 8, 2011

I recently signed up with an electric company for my house. In California, you get a monthly bill sent to your house, and I assumed it would be the same here in New Zealand.

I was told over the phone by the electric company employee, "If you want a bill mailed to your house, you have to pay a $150 bond. We have a new system if you do not want to pay $150 to get a bill; you will be mailed a letter that will be red, yellow, or green. If it's green, that means you have enough credit, and you don't have to pay anything to keep your electricity on. If it's yellow, that means that you're running out of credit and need to add more money to your account. If it's red, that means you have run out of credit and need to top up at the shop."

SATURDAY, JULY 9, 2011

Grant and I went for a really long hike in Karekare. After dinner and a fire, we drank whiskey and ginger beer while lying on the ground by the fire. We joked about doing this every year for the rest of our lives, asking each other, "Where do we go from here?"

We're trying to find countries we can both be in. We were thinking South America, Asia, or looking into volunteer programs, trying to find some alternative country that we both can be in that is not so expensive.

We don't feel as tense and stressed out, but we still don't know what we're doing. We're going to visit both our families in California in October. His parents are going to be in San Francisco visiting his brother at the end of October, and we'll meet them there, see his brother, sister-in-law, and nephew, and visit my family too.

We may or may not come back in November because Grant's visa is up at the end of October. It depends on if Grant can get another temporary visa until my visa is up in March. If he can get another visa, we may come back and work until the new year, or until my visa is up.

171

Grant wants to go back to Scotland and get a master's degree in landscape architecture. We haven't been together long enough to apply for a partnership visa in each other's countries.

We're not sure what to do next. We know we want to be together. We know we don't want two winters. We want to tour the South Island and parts of Australia. We want to go back to school. My temp jobs have made it abundantly clear that I need more education under my belt to be qualified to do something else. There are lots of programs that I will apply for in Scotland. We won't be able to start school until fall 2012.

We're trying to figure out what to do and where to do it between now and then.

SUNDAY, JULY 10, 2011

Grant and I went to the Japanese restaurant Renkon on Durham Lane in Auckland. We sat outside and ate chicken katsu.

Out of nowhere, a man sat down with us and acted like he knew us. I didn't recognize him, and Grant didn't look like he did either. We made polite conversation, hoping we would be able to place our mystery guest.
It finally clicked when he said he was trying to sell his beer at the bar neighboring Renkon. It was our old, weird neighbor from the first place we lived together pushing his home brew. Our old neighbor has an odd way about him—he's the poster child for the dangers of home

brewing.

Then he left with his beer and wandered farther up the alley and went up a staircase.

Then Grant said, "What the hell…" looking at the alley behind me where our old neighbor went down.

I turned around to see an angry-looking man sprinting down the alley.

"Who's that?"

"I don't know. I saw our old neighbor run down the stairs, and then a few seconds later that angry guy ran down the stairs and chased him down the alley."

"I'm so glad we don't live there anymore."

MONDAY, JULY 11, 2011

This was my first week with the on-call after-hours phone that rang The Muppet's "Mahna Mahna" nonstop.

I received multiple calls about the locations of light switches and heaters in the venues from the call center on behalf of customers. The call center and the customers have the same maps as I do.

After multiple calls wanting me to "shed light on the situation," I granted them permission to send an electrician to turn on the lights for the customer. The venue was in a suburb I have never been in. I told the call-center worker, "I don't know what else to tell you. I have never been to this venue; I don't even know where Panmure is. You have the same map as me, and so does the customer. I don't know what to say other than the light switches are on all of the walls."

TUESDAY, JULY 12, 2011

Everything is upside down and back to front in New Zealand. We're lucky to have a washer and dryer in our house, but they aren't like any washer or dryer I've ever seen. Neither of them have a stop or a start button, instead there's a dial with a picture of a sun or half a sun for settings.

They are placed in the bathroom next to the bathtub, which is also the main entrance to our house. When you go through our front door, you enter the bathroom, and to the left is the washer and dryer.

The dryer was installed upside down on the ceiling, hanging up above the washing machine. I have trouble reaching my dangling, upside-down dryer when I'm putting my wet clothes in.

Last night, Grant said, "I put the clothes in the dryer on the low setting."

"There is no 'low.' Do you mean you put the dryer on 'half sun?'"

The washing machine only has a dial with numbers that are out of numerical order and accompanied by a square diagram with numbers that are out of numerical order. We were told by our landlord that "the washing machine seems like it's not doing anything a lot of the time during the washing cycle, but it is, just let it do its thing."

It takes over an hour and a half to wash the clothes. Most of the time, it does absolutely nothing: no water going in or out, no spinning. The door locks once it is started, and it doesn't allow you to open the door for at least fifteen minutes after it has finished washing the clothes.

WEDNESDAY, JULY 13, 2011

I've been trying to create a positive work environment and be extra nice to Gretchen, the girl who still wears her dead dog's collar around her neck. Since our boss Selma is away sick today, I told Gretchen to look for a job with animals online today. Since she loves animals so much, she should look for jobs at the zoo or working with animals, like bathing dogs.

Gretchen said, "I've always wanted a car that I could bathe animals in."

"You should totally look for a dog-bather job. I think you would be good at it."

She began looking for jobs online and a few moments later, she said, "Here's a job that pays eighteen to twenty-five dollars an hour. But a main part of the job is transporting dead pets."

"What would you have to do?"

"Transport dead pets. I think I would like it better if they were alive. I want to pet them, and I think they would be too stiff for me if they were dead."

The job was advertised as pre-crematorium, and she seemed surprised that she'd have to deal with dead animals.

She continued looking online for work with live animals. "Here's one: whale hygienist. I reckon whales have good hygiene. Except they eat plankton."

SATURDAY, JULY 16, 2011

Grant and I have been collecting driftwood on the beach to make fires in the fireplace. Our place looks lovely, but like all the houses I've lived in in New Zealand, it isn't insulated. We can see our breath inside, even with the fire going. Our toothpaste is frozen solid, and bananas on the kitchen counter are turning black from freezing.

MONDAY, JULY 18, 2011

I told Gretchen, "Your sandwich smells good."

"It was, it's all gone down, but I'll still eat my dinner. My flatmates reckon I have worms because I eat so much.

They're boys, and I eat more than them. When I'm hungry,
I tell them I'm feeding my worms."

TUESDAY, JULY 19, 2011

On the bus to work, I read in a Buddhist magazine the
quote, "Iron, when heated in the flames and pounded,
becomes a fine sword. The flaws in iron come to the
surface when it is forged. A strong sword is made by
pounding a piece of hot iron and bringing out its
impurities. Likewise, we can develop an unbreakable, solid
self by squarely confronting and overcoming obstacles."

The second I came through the door this morning, my
boss Selma jumped up from her desk and came at me and
screamed in my face, "You and Gretchen keep making the
same mistakes over and over. I'm going to pound the
information into your thick head over and over until you
get it." As she screamed, she pounded her fist into her
hand. "Do you understand?"

She was almost quoting the magazine word for word. I
almost started laughing as she screamed in my face because
I knew it had nothing to do with the job or her. It was like
she was a messenger: "You're doing it again; you're being
complacent. When will you learn you need to value your
talent and challenge yourself?"

WEDNESDAY, JULY 20, 2011

"I have to close your blinds now; the sun is rotating

around the building," Gretchen told me.

"No, the earth is rotating around the sun."

"Naw, the sun was shining in the other window earlier today, and now it is shining in yours. So we're both right."

THURSDAY, JULY 21, 2011

My experiences at Auckland Council have made it abundantly clear that I need additional education to qualify for better jobs. I've been e-mailing universities in Scotland to see if I can do some sort of certificate program in graphic design. I got this response today from one university:

> Dear Jamie,
>
> Due to changes in the Tier 4 rules set by the UK Border Agency, we are unable to accept any applications from outside the UK.
>
> Apologies for any inconvenience caused.
>
> Regards, Admissions

What are we supposed to do? Where are we supposed to go, and how? Grant's visa is up in October.

SATURDAY, JULY 22, 2011

This morning, my boss Selma Shark had a one-on-one meeting with me. She is either screaming at me or Gretchen. Selma asked me, "How are you doing?"

Other than walking on eggshells at work, I'm counting down the minutes until my contract is up September 30— eight weeks, one day, and counting. I said, "I have the flu. I feel terrible. This morning I put my dress on inside out and then backward. I managed to put it on the right way, but now the tie is in the front, but I had to get to work this morning, so this is how I left the house."

My eyes were puffy since I had just woken up. I took nighttime cold medicine last night, which put me in a coma, and I had trouble getting up this morning. I fell asleep with wet hair last night, and it seemed to have molded into the shape of my boyfriend's armpit, where I sleep at night. Parts were sticking up, and other sections were matted down.

Tearing up and wiping my dripping nose, I continued, "My boyfriend's visa is up in October, and we're trying to figure out how to go back to Scotland together. We thought I could go under a student visa, but they just changed a law, and one of the schools I contacted said they are no longer taking applications from outside the UK."

"Can he go back to the US with you?"

"Only for ninety days. It's incredibly complicated. It's really hard to be away from both our families, and we want

179

to be together."

"I tell you what, go visit your family, but New Zealand is the best place for you to be right now, given the state the world is in right now."

"Yeah, because it's so isolated, it's not really affected by the recession."

"That, and I am a woman of the lord. It says in the scriptures that, because of people's sins, the earth will begin spitting back at us. That's why there are so many natural disasters right now, like earthquakes and volcanoes erupting, and that is why America is in the state that it is in now, because of all the sins and lies that have been happening there."

"I guess New Zealand hasn't had any natural disasters until Christchurch."

"How long have you and your boyfriend been together?"

"We met New Year's Eve." And we are currently living in sin. I'm now wondering if she thinks my American sinning in New Zealand caused the earthquake in Christchurch. He rocked my world, but there is no way we could have rocked the earth.

"Are there any other things that you need to be trained with?"

"The problem is, I don't know I'm doing things wrong until bad things happen. Like with the notice-board schedules, I've been following the same instructions I was given in May, and just this week you told me the instructions are wrong, and because I ran the schedule incorrectly and e-mailed the schedule to the wrong people, you said, 'It cost the Council three thousand dollars this week.' I'm surprised this hasn't happened before."

"Yeah, and the system crashing cost Council thirty-five thousand dollars."

"What? That wasn't my fault."

"Yes, it was. I wasn't going to bring it up, but it's your fault. You did something in the Protege program that caused the system to crash. It cost thirty-five thousand dollars to send out security guards and technicians to fix everything."

"I didn't even know that was possible. How did I do that?"

What did she mean she wasn't going to bring it up? If it's true that I cost the Council thirty-five thousand dollars a couple weeks ago and three thousand dollars this week, totaling more than double my yearly salary, why wouldn't she tell me? She yells at me about everything, why not this? Maybe this is why her boss has been glaring at me?

"I didn't know it was possible either or how you did it, but you did," she said casually.

"Shouldn't we find out from the technicians what I did to cause this problem so I can make sure I don't do it again and train everyone else not to do it too? It seems crazy to me that I could have unknowingly caused the system to crash."

"Don't worry about it, I wasn't going to tell you. It doesn't matter because you're never going to do it again."

"But if neither of us knows how I did it, how will I know not to do it again? What if someone else does it too by accident? Don't you think we should ask the technicians how it happened?"

"Don't worry about it; you're never going to do it again."

SATURDAY, JULY 23, 2011

We tried to watch Disorder, a zombie love story directed by Thomas Sainsbury, but it was sold out.

SUNDAY, JULY 24, 2011

Grant and I went to a pizza place near our house last night. We're both stressed out, hating our jobs, and worried about Grant's visa expiring in October. We ordered a Mediterranean calzone, but it hardly had any filling. There were only small pieces of feta and vegetables widely spaced between thick dough.

"I don't know what this is, but it's not a calzone," I complained to Grant.

"So, how are you?"

"I'm really stressed out and don't know what we're going to do, and I think this is the worst meal of my life."

Grant laughed, "We can always get hitched in Vegas!"

I wasn't sure if he was joking or proposing. I'm still fundamentally confused as to why Grant even likes me, much less loves me and wants to live with me. Since he's divorced, I didn't think he would want to get married again and never considered it an option. But if he was being serious, it made me mad. I looked at him closely and sharply said, "Are you joking?"

He just smiled.

"Don't do that over this," I snapped as I waved my hand over our funky calzone.

Grant apologized, and we spent the rest of dinner quiet and awkwardly looking at each other. After dinner, I took Grant to the beach near our house. I sat on a tree branch and told him, "This is my favorite place in New Zealand. I will say "yes" if you ask me properly."

He didn't get the hint to ask me there. He just said, "I'm sorry, I should get a ring."

"I don't need a ring."

"No, I'm sorry. I should have asked you properly.

183

MONDAY, JULY 25, 2011

Selma spent the morning yelling at Gretchen and then left at noon.

Gretchen said, "I've never gotten into so much trouble in my life, not even by my mum. When I was a child, I was very angry, and no one could control me. My mum sent me to my dad's house, he sent me back to my mum's, and then she sent me to my aunt's. I hated it at my aunt's house, so I burned down my bedroom there."

"What! Why?" I was trying to eat an apple as she told this story. I began choking and gave the referee time-out signal. I was crying from laughing so hard, and so was Susie, who had moved her chair closer so that she could listen to the story.

"My aunt liked to walk around the house naked, and she was a very big lady. I was only eight, and I hated it and used to hide under my bed. So I burned my room down. When the fire brigade came in, I started crying because all I wanted was my teddy bear. My uncle, who was not my real uncle, who is a panel beater, had to hold me back."

"What's a panel beater?"

"Someone who repairs cars."

The very big lady in the cubicle next to us did not like this story and told us, "Keep it down, please."

TUESDAY, JULY 26, 2011

Every Tuesday I seem to have a meltdown after work.
Selma is screaming at me so much, most days I go home
and sit on the ground and shake. Grant and I are now
calling Tuesdays, "Meltdown Tuesdays."

WEDNESDAY, JULY 27, 2011

Selma left work early after screaming at me and Gretchen
while Susie awkwardly sat in the corner. After Selma left,
Gretchen excitedly said, "Guess what, Jamie, today I
applied for a job at the zoo! I updated my cover letter this
morning, saying I would die without animals."

"Cool, what job is it?"

"Trainee zookeeper working with reptiles and
invertebrates—whatever the hell an invertebrate is."

"You should probably find out before the interview. Look
it up online."

After a quick Google search, she read from Wikipedia,
"'An invertebrate is an animal (a multicellular eukaryote)
without a backbone. Fish, amphibians, reptiles, birds, and
mammals.' So, like fish." With her accent, she pronounced
fish like "fush."

A few moments later, Gretchen said, "The other day I was
watching the news, and there was a penguin, and it was
cold enough for him to enjoy a swim."

185

THURSDAY, JULY 28, 2011

This morning, Gretchen told me that she and her boyfriend are planning to start trying to have kids. She said that she has been getting Depo-Provera shots for the past ten years so that she doesn't get a period. She said she "didn't like having period cramps."

She also told me, "I'm scared that the weight of the baby will snap me in half. What if my body just gives way?"

"What are you talking about? Your body isn't designed to do that."

"Have you ever had a leg cramp? The other night I had a leg cramp in my calf, and I just pointed my toe and kept it like that for a really long time. Once I had a leg cramp in both calves. I wouldn't wish that pain on anyone."

"Leg cramps are normal. I hear one out of ten women have orgasms when they give birth. Maybe you will be one of them."

FRIDAY, JULY 29, 2011

Selma Shark hasn't been in since Tuesday. Susie still hasn't been trained on how to do anything. I know it's not nice, but I talk to Gretchen and then write up little stories about what she told me and e-mail them to Susie. Gretchen sits in between me and Susie. Susie's desk is in the corner and far enough away that she can't hear our conversations. This week, Susie's been laughing in the corner while reading the stories I've been sending her, and Gretchen has just been looking confused.

SUNDAY, JULY 30, 2011

I'm not sure if we're engaged or not. Grant says he has a secret plan for us to be able to live in the same country together, but he won't tell me what it is. He's had the flu all week; he calls it "lurgy" and has mostly been asleep when I've seen him. I'm not sure if I should poke this sweaty, feverish Scottish man I'm sharing a bed with and ask if we're engaged.

MONDAY, AUGUST 1, 2011

We had a team meeting. Our boss Selma talked at us for over an hour about how she doesn't mean to scream when she talks to us, and she knows how stressful the job is because she has been in the job for over ten years and has seen many people come and go because of the stress.

I asked, "What has kept you here for ten years?" She seems to hate the job more than we do.

"My husband had an accident and has brain damage and has been out of work for over a few years."

As if she had the right answer in class, Gretchen's hand shot up, "Oh! I think I have that!"

All eyes turned to Gretchen as she explained why she

thought she had brain damage, "When I was a little girl, like seven, I was roller-skating and going really fast. My mum said, 'Gretchen, Gretchen, slow down,' but I didn't listen. I fell down and smacked the back of my head on the ground real hard. I started crying and said, 'My head hurts,' but my mum didn't listen. We went to my grandparents' house, and I was still crying that my head hurt, and they told me to be quiet and lay down. I lay down for a while, and when I got up there was a big pool of blood on my pillow. I reckon I have brain damage."

I gasped, "You've had a lot of physical trauma as a child!"

"Yeah, when I was eight, I got hit by a car. This lady was going around a bus real fast, and I was crossing the street, and she hit me. You know when you hit an animal you don't have to stop? Well, she must have thought she hit an animal, so she didn't stop when she hit me. Since I was so little, I flew across the street and landed in the bus stop. This bone," she pointed to her hip, "went across my tummy, and I broke my pelvis and tailbone. I laid in a pool of blood in the bus stop, and there were all of these kids around staring. You know they did a mural for me cause of that. You know that mural of the bowling pins flying up in the air from the bowling ball that says, 'Don't get bowled. Look both ways' on the corner? That's cause of me. There's still a blood stain on the ground there."

TUESDAY, AUGUST 2, 2011

This morning I asked Gretchen, "How are you today?"

She rubbed her belly and said, "Oh, I have my morning pains."

"Your family seems to have a lot of stomach problems."

"Yeah, my mum has a giant scar on her stomach from waking up during surgery from getting her appendix out, and my brother has been constipated for over eight years."

"What? Your brother hasn't pooed for eight years? How's that possible? How old is he?"

"He's ten. No, he has pooed. It's just after he was potty trained when he was two, he only poos in his pants now."

"That's not constipation, that's something else. You should take him to the doctor."

"We have. He has ADHD. He's so hyper when he comes over to my house; I just lock him in the bathroom."

"I guess that's a good place to keep him with his condition."

WEDNESDAY, AUGUST 3, 2011

This afternoon Gretchen listed off all of the animals that bit her and how.

"Once I got bitten by a dog on the ankle when I was midair, and it hurt really bad. I still have a scar. See?" she said as she pulled up her pant leg.

"What?" I couldn't help but laugh.

"Don't laugh, it really hurt, there was so much blood."

"I'm sorry, I didn't mean to laugh, it's just that no one has ever told me that they were bitten by a dog midair. How did that happen?"

"Me and my boyfriend were play fighting, and he threw me up in the air. While I was in the air, a dog thought we were really fighting and bit me on the ankle. The dog punctured an artery or something, there was so much blood, and we were really far away from the hospital. By the time my boyfriend's aunt wrapped up my ankle, it was completely filled with blood, and she had to rewrap it."

She then said, "Ducks bite really hard. It hurts when you get bitten by a duck."

"Why were ducks biting you?"

"When I was working at animal welfare, there were these ducks that had botulism, and I had to shove tubes down their throat to give them medicine, and they would bite me. There once was a goose there that I had to give medicine to also."

She continued to talk about geese bites, "Have you ever been to Western Springs Park? There are a lot of real big geese there that chase you and bite you. There are giant eels in the water there too."

"Eels?"

"Yeah, freshwater eels are in all of the creeks and streams here in New Zealand. When I was kid, we would catch eels. They have a coating on them, so they are really hard to catch because they are so slippery. But we would catch them and put them in a bucket."

"What would you do with them?"

"We wouldn't eat them or anything, we would just stare at them or stab them."

"Huh?"

"Boy, it was real fun being a kid."

THURSDAY, AUGUST 4, 2011

This afternoon Gretchen was commenting on how I use different words than she does because I'm American. She said, "I watch a lot of American TV, and it's weird, all the different words you use."

"Yeah, I thought it was weird how you guys call the woods or nature, 'the bush.' That means something else in America."

"What, like George Bush's house?"

"No, something that is not office appropriate."

"Whatever, I'm not office appropriate," Gretchen said.

191

FRIDAY, AUGUST 5, 2011

Grant still has the flu, and I'm still not sure if we're engaged, but I looked at rings at the Diamond Shop with Susie on our lunch break. I found one that I really like. It's a small, round diamond with tiny diamonds circling it and a thin band with tiny diamonds.

SATURDAY, AUGUST 6, 2011

Grant seems to be recovered from the flu. I asked him, "I know you have a secret plan, but if it involves paperwork of any kind that needs approval from different countries, we should probably start filling out papers. Those things can take a while to get approved."

Grant looked tired from work and said, "This isn't very romantic, but I was hoping you would come to Scotland with me as a fiancée."

SUNDAY, AUGUST 7, 2011

I didn't think I was ever going to get married or even need a ring. Now that it seems I'm engaged and found a ring I like, it's all I can think about. I feel like Gollum thinking about the ring and rubbing my bare ring finger. My fingers are too small for the ring I like to be resized. It has to be custom made and will take four weeks to make.

MONDAY, AUGUST 8, 2011

Selma Shark is out sick again. Gretchen and I have been job hunting. Gretchen was looking for more animal-related jobs, most of which required a degree relating to animals or science. I asked Gretchen, "Why don't you go back to school? You can learn how to wash dogs and work as a dog groomer."

"Naw, I left school, and I'm never going back."

"How far did you make it in school?"

"Fifth form."

"We have different terms in America. What age is that?"

"Fifteen. What is fifteen in America?"

"Fifteen."

TUESDAY, AUGUST 9, 2011

Joke e-mails circulate around the office; today Gretchen was looking at America's shame: a people-of-Walmart e-mail.

The e-mail had horrifying pictures of crazy, fat Americans wearing too little with too much to cover. Gretchen said, "You might like this place, Walmart?"

I just rolled my eyes, "Have you ever been to Walmart?"

"I've never been out of the country before. I took a train to the South Island once."

"What? You took a train to the South Island? Do you mean a boat?"

"Naw, I took a train. I went to Wellington."

"Wellington's on the North Island."

"Never mind, I've never been off the North Island."

WEDNESDAY, AUGUST 10, 2011

Gretchen came up to me panting, "Jamie, can I borrow your Chap Stick? My lips are so dry my mouth hurts." As she said this, she pulled on her lips.

Lips shining with a thick coat of gloss, I lied, "Sorry, I left mine at home today. Why don't you drink some water?"

"It burns when I drink water; that's how chapped my lips are." She was propping herself up on my desk as she continued to pant and beg me to let her use my Chap Stick.

Selma ended up letting Gretchen use her Chap Stick. As Gretchen coated her lips with our boss's gloss, Gretchen said, "Thanks, I get cold sores a lot."

SATURDAY, AUGUST 13, 2011

When I woke up this morning, I realized we were out of milk and toothpaste. Frustrated from squeezing the last bits of toothpaste out for the past few weeks, all I wanted to do was properly brush my teeth after I drank my coffee.

I rolled out of bed, threw on one of Grant's sweatshirts, and walked outside on my quest for milk and toothpaste. As soon as I shut the door behind me, I realized I didn't have my house key or my phone. Grant was working in the North Shore and wouldn't be home for the next seven hours, and our landlords were out of town for three weeks. I was locked out of the house, with sleep crust in my eyes and desperately needing coffee and to brush my teeth.

"Fuck, what do I do?" I said to myself aloud as I tried the door that was locked behind me. I walked through the muddy side of the house and was surprised to find the living room windows were much higher off the ground than I realized; they were a few feet above my head.

The neighbor's fence was about four feet from the house wall, and I'm just over five feet tall. I climbed halfway up the fence, standing on my toes, and tried to reach the windows. I managed to get one of the windows open with my fingertips and yanked open the curtain, leaving a muddy handprint. The only problem I had now was getting up to the height of the window.

I contemplated how badly I would get hurt if I slipped while trying to get through the window. The top of the fence was around eight feet up, and the space between me on the fence and the window was around four feet. I reached across the empty space, eight feet up in the air, gripping the windowsill tightly, toes on the fence, butt in the air, and limbs shaking. There was no other option now; I'd gone too far. I told myself if I did fall I would most likely not die because the ground was soft and muddy. Worst-case scenario: I would break a limb and hopefully be found by Grant in seven hours.

I managed to tumble through the window and not crack my head open on the dining-room table on the other side of the window. My heart was racing, I was breathing heavily, and I looked down out the window at the muddy ground far below the window. I impressed myself with my ninja skills.

This is why I will never leave the house again without drinking coffee.

MONDAY, AUGUST 15, 2011

Gretchen had an interview for a job working with animals yesterday. I asked her, "How did your interview go at the pony-ride place?"

"It was OK. A donkey talked to me," she said casually.

"What did it say?"

"I don't know. Donkeys talk like, "Naaaaa, naaaaa." It was quiet all day, but when it saw me it started talking. When I was at the zoo, donkeys talked to me there too. There are lots of donkeys at the zoo. Maybe it was a camel."

WEDNESDAY, AUGUST 17, 2011

How come I have multiple customers not wanting to confirm bookings until the full moon? How is this a normal request?

Why do I have more than one person calling and saying, "I can't tell you which day I want the venue until we can see the full moon."

Are they planning their werewolf meeting?

SATURDAY, AUGUST 19, 2011

Last night we had a very odd night out with a group of friends who we awkwardly told we were engaged. They were all looking at my bare ring finger. The ring is still being made. Rightfully, they were concerned we were rushing into things.

I had brunch with Grant's female friend who is very concerned about our engagement because Grant is divorced. She's a bit older than I am, in Grant's age bracket, and understandably worried for us both, as she moved to New Zealand after breaking off an engagement of her own.

After a while, I had to interrupt her and say, "I really appreciate what you're telling me. I understand what you're saying about how horrible it feels to be engaged to the wrong person. I've done that before too. It feels different when you're engaged to the right person. I think all of my experiences of feeling what it felt like to be with the wrong guys helps give me wisdom about what it feels to be with the right person. I hope you feel that way someday too."

SUNDAY, AUGUST 21, 2011

So far our engagement has consisted of having uncomfortable conversations with friends and filling out a huge form for my fiancée visa. For every question we answer, we have to have physical evidence to prove it, like when we met and that we've been living together, such as e-mails, letters, photographs, bank statements, and tenancy agreements. All documents need to be original and can't be photocopied. Both of our passports and original birth certificates need to be processed in Manila, where the New Zealand branch of the UK Border Agency office is.

MONDAY, AUGUST 22, 2011

I asked my boss Selma if I could please have a day off to go to Immigration to get mandatory biometric testing done for my visa to the UK. Selma screamed at me all morning. She demanded I call Immigration to ask how long the testing would take.

Cowering beneath her screaming at me, I said, "It costs three dollars and thirty cents a minute to call. I can't afford to make the call."

"No. That's wrong. It can't be three dollars and thirty cents a minute, it's only down the street."

This doesn't seem that unreasonable a price in New Zealand where it costs $5 for a single cucumber or bell pepper at the grocery store, a decent cocktail costs $20, a beer is $10, limes are $29.99 per kilogram, it costs 20 cents to send a text message, and it's so expensive per minute to talk on your cell phone that no ever calls anyone.

"It's three dollars and thirty cents a minute. Look, it says it on the website and the e-mail that they sent me, saying I need to get biometric testing done."

"No! That's wrong! I don't believe that! Call them from our phones here! You can't take a day off!"

The phones at Council wouldn't let me make the phone call since it cost $3.30 a minute. Selma didn't believe me, and the conversation above repeated itself over and over and over for the rest of the morning. Eventually, Selma, probably because her voice was going hoarse, picked up the phone and tried to call and couldn't get through either, so she finally believed me.

Gretchen, who is still wearing her dead dog's collar around her neck, wrote and passed me a note, "I think I need to go to the doctor right now, but I am too afraid to ask."

"What's wrong with you?"

"I'm too embarrassed to tell you."

"What's wrong?"

"I was just in the toilet and thought I got my period, but then I realized it was coming from behind instead of the front. I think I need to go to a doctor right now, but I think I'll get in trouble for asking."

"You should go to the doctor, that's not normal."

"It only happens when I go to the toilet."

"That should never happen. You should go to the doctor. Seriously, go."

Gretchen sat in the cubicle next to me, in between me and my screaming boss the rest of the day, bleeding out of her ass, too afraid to say she needed to go to the doctor. She was more scared of our boss than the fact that her ass was bleeding.

When Selma was at lunch, I wrote Nam Myoho Renge Kyo down on a piece of paper and handed it to Gretchen. I told her, "You know how I practice Buddhism? Well, this is what I chant. It will help with your stress. You really should go to a doctor and get some help."

WEDNESDAY, AUGUST 24, 2011

Last night I had a nightmare that I was about to get anally raped at work by a man who was commanded to do so by

Selma, who was standing next to him screaming, "These are your options!"

I ended up only getting half a day off, which was not enough time to get everything done. Yesterday Gretchen called in sick and came back today with a perm, saying, "I don't feel right. I got a perm yesterday, and I think the chemicals leaked into my brain. I couldn't work yesterday because I had a foot cramp. It hurt so bad I couldn't walk."

I spent another week being screamed at and crying in the toilets, the elevators, by the copy machine, at my desk, and on all of my breaks. I've had overwhelming anxiety. I've been finding it hard to breathe, and my stomach has been hurting. I wake up most nights with nightmares about my job and getting yelled at by my boss. I wake up exhausted, not wanting to get out bed. I lie in bed staring at the ceiling, knowing it's not a nightmare, that I can't escape when I wake up, and it's my reality. I have to get up and go work, and my nightmare is Monday to Friday, forty hours a week.

I didn't think it could get worse than my last temp job where I sat next to a crazy mime who said he wanted to cut off my arm with a machete and drink my blood, and text messaged pictures of his dick to girls in the office. At least he stopped talking to me after I screamed, "You're a dick," in the middle of the cubicles because he'd said horrible, racist things.

I cried by myself on my last break today after spending the day shaking in my cubicle. Cubicles are weird places.

201

Instead of post-traumatic stress disorder, I think I have present-traumatic temping disorder.

THURSDAY, AUGUST 25, 2011

I watched the Love/Hate Monologues with Cyan tonight. Her little sister Lyla is staying with her for a while. They are both so beautiful and sweet.

SUNDAY, AUGUST 28, 2011

The ring was finally finished. Our friends seem more comfortable with the engagement. Everyone's saying they'll come to Scotland for the wedding. We sent the visa application early this week. It's scary to send away all the documents you have proving your identity while you're in a foreign country, including my passport. Since it's being processed in Manila, I'm chanting for my visa application to only be in Manila for one day and for them to instantly approve it and mail it back the same day.

TUESDAY, AUGUST 30, 2011

Selma's away sick today, so Gretchen and I looked at wedding dresses online. I also looked up castles in Scotland. There are so many castles there. Friends and family at home are asking us when and where we'll be getting married. My fiancée visa will only allow me to be in the UK for six months and only allow me to marry Grant. I'll have to apply for a different visa to stay in Scotland and

202

work once we're married.

I've never been to Scotland, so it's basically impossible for me to know where in Scotland I want to get married. It's not a very big country, but there are hundreds of castles to choose from. As I've learned as a venue reservations coordinator, you have to work with the availability of the venue more than a date you would like. Hopefully it will be easier to make plans once we get there.

THURSDAY, SEPTEMBER 1, 2011

I watched three short films Thomas Sainsbury made called Jerry Pearl Plimpton.

SUNDAY, SEPTEMBER 4, 2011

Since visas, plane tickets, and weddings cost money that I don't really have, I've been chanting for more money. I still have a car I'm paying off parked at my mom's house. It doesn't seem logical to keep it. My friend Grace in California totaled her car, and she got a loan to buy a new car for $10,000. I told her if she wanted mine to go knock on my mom's door, who will hand her my keys. It should be enough money to pay off the remainder of my car loan, flights, visas, and a little cushion while I wait for my marriage visa to go through.

MONDAY, SEPTEMBER 5, 2011

The Rugby World Cup starts this Friday. There's a

competition decorating the office for the World Cup. Whichever cubicle team wins wins nothing. The venue-reservations team got Australia, so we have to decorate our cubicles like Australia.

Last week, I asked Selma's boss if she could go to anger-management classes. It's like walking through a mine field working here—you never know what will set her off. The pressure is on to make our cubicles look the best.

Selma has ordered us to win the office-decorating competition. Hands shaking, Gretchen and I are cutting out as many cute and cuddly animals as we can find. I have turned my cubicle into Koala Wala Land. I have printed out, in color, hundreds of different sizes of the same picture of two koalas sitting in a tree branch. I connected the branches and made a giant tree filled with koalas covering the wall to the ceiling.

This job has made me a nervous wreck; all I can do to cope is cut and paste cute little koalas, creating koala wallpaper. As I'm making it, I'm thinking, "Gosh, my cubicle looks like a room that you see in movies, where crazy people put things all over the walls. I wonder what the new person will think when they replace me when my contract is up."

TUESDAY, SEPTEMBER 6, 2011

After spending the morning actually working doing bond refunds, invoicing customers, and other boring office stuff, my boss Selma said, "Are you going to do more decorating? We have to win!"

Only Selma can turn something fun into something stressful. How can we decorate more? No one else in the office has decorated at all. At all. Not even a map or a flag. I have koala wallpaper. We printed out two maps of Australia four feet high by four feet wide on the blueprint printer. We have printed out hundreds of Australian creatures—kangaroos, sharks, snakes, spiders, shrimp, crocodiles—and we've made a mini shrine for Steve Erwin, the Crocodile Hunter. I imagine we've killed roughly three trees with all of the printing we've done.

Gretchen has brought in everything possible to go camping with, including a portable solar shower, a real barbecue, flashlight, and all of her boogie boarding gear consisting of a giant, green boogie board, flippers, and snorkel gear. We have green-and-gold streamers and balloons all over the office, and five Australian flags.

Gretchen asked me, "Do you want some sunflower seeds?"

Gretchen opened up a cooler that she also brought to work; it was completely filled with sunflower seeds. I reached my hand in and put some in my mouth. They tasted stale. "Why do you have so many sunflower seeds?"

"They're my dead parrot's old food. They're not too old; we just bought them earlier this year."

Eating dead-parrot sunflower seeds while frantically

cutting out pictures of koalas to avoid being screamed at by my boss equals Tuesday for me. Where's my visa?

WEDNESDAY, SEPTEMBER 7, 2011

There's a really bad smell coming from the fridge at work, and everyone has been complaining about it for the past several weeks. Today after someone was complaining about the smell, I said, "It's the smell of all the souls dying from the people in the cubicles."

THURSDAY, SEPTEMBER 8, 2011

While riding the elevator with other people in the office, there is always an awkward silence. Me and a middle-aged lady were riding the elevator silently together. We glanced at each other. She said, "I'm tired. I'm ready to go home."

"Yeah, me too. I'm waiting for a visa to come through so I can leave the country."

"OK," she said slowly and rolled her eyes at me like I have really lost the plot.

I have lost the plot. I'm scaring people in elevators.

FRIDAY, SEPTEMBER 9, 2011

Yesterday was so bad. This job is so bad. Selma was

screaming at Gretchen all morning about a gas leak in one of the venues, which is obviously not her fault. She had had a sore stomach all morning from stress; I can only assume that Selma is stressing out Gretchen and causing her anal bleeding.

We are booking venues—crappy, cheap, dirty venues with sticky floors and puke in the sink—for idiots to use for their weddings, twenty-first birthdays, and business meetings. One of the venues is used as a day care, and every day we get e-mails complaining about a homeless man who lives and shits on the back deck.

Selma screams at us, standing with her hands on her hips, her icy eyes piercing down on us, her mouth open showing too many teeth, like a shark. Her teeth are rotten and blackened from decades of smoking. You can feel the heat of her breath on your neck, and it smells like something has died in her mouth. Selma screams until she shakes, sweating and exhausted by her anger.

Everyone in the office sees, but no one does anything. They just stare at me over the cubicle walls. I look up at them with tears brimming from my eyes, hoping they will do something, say something—anything. But they do nothing.

Her boss is the only male on the office floor. He acts like he has no balls. He can hear her screaming; sometimes he will stand next to her as she screams and just look panicked. When I asked him if my boss could go to anger-management classes, he said, "I'm sure she's not angry; she is just very direct." Get your head out of your ass and do something, you ball-less asshole.

This isn't me complaining, "Oh, I don't like my job, it's boring." My job is so bad it has caused me to shake and have panic attacks and nightmares, and my coworker Gretchen to have anal bleeding from stress.

My last weeks in Auckland shouldn't be spent being screamed at in a cubicle by a religious fanatic. I've been here since July 2010 and I've worked nonstop—in a basement smelling like rotten cabbage, an agency for ex-cons, and a room filled with twenty-something American-hating international temps. I've worked next to a perverted, racist, psychotic mime that wanted to machete my arm off and drink my blood. And now I'm making koala wallpaper while being screamed at and fed dead-parrot bird food.

This isn't normal.

I'm done.

Today I got to work, knowing it would be my last day and thinking how funny it would be to spend the day knowing it without anyone else knowing. But I had already told Gretchen that today was my last day, and that she should quit too. I walked into the office as usual. Selma said, "Gretchen is away sick, and it's going to be just me and you today."

I said, "OK," and went to the kitchen to get water. As I filled up my glass, I thought, "I'm not going to be spending one more day getting screamed at by this vicious cunt. You can't polish a turd. I quit."

I walked back to my desk, and Selma was walking to the kitchen. I took a picture of my koala wallpaper and packed up my stuff. I told Judith, the office gossip, "It was nice knowing you. I quit."

Judith gossips about everyone, so I figured that would be the fastest way to spread the word. She thought I was joking and started to laugh. As I walked away, she said, "Are you serious? You are leaving? Does anyone know?"

"Nope. I got my visa back yesterday and sold my car in America for ten thousand dollars. I was going to stay one more day, but I don't see the point. I don't need this shit."

Then I stuck up both my middle fingers, flipped off Judith, and walked out.

Judith's jaw dropped, and her sagging face swayed in slow motion. She just about fell out of her seat to spread this juicy gossip.

I walked down the street to Matador Temp Agency and ran into Susie. I told her, "I quit. I would be disrespecting myself to stay a minute longer."

I told the maniacally bubbly receptionist, "I quit my job. What forms do I need to fill out?"

I filled out three pieces of paper. My temp consultant raced across the office from the elevator, avoiding eye contact with me. She didn't help me with the mime, and she knew I was being screamed at by Selma. I walked out, telling the receptionist, "Have a nice day."

I walked home. A different recruiter, the chocolate/chalkboard interviewer from Matador, called me and demanded to know what happened today. I told her, "I walked out. I don't care. I'm leaving the country. I filled out my final papers. Is there anything else that needs to be done to get my money?"

She was less than impressed with my exit, saying I was unprofessional and supposed to be representing Matador.

I said, "My boss is crazy. She thinks natural disasters are caused by Americans sinning and seriously needs to go to anger-management classes. In my last job, there was a crazy guy sitting next to me and sending pictures of his dick to girls in the office. I filed a formal complaint with HR with three girls and told Matador, and they were just like, 'Sorry, there are no other jobs.' Then at this job, my boss is insane, screaming constantly, and I'm sitting next to a girl wearing her dead dog's collar around her neck. I may have been unprofessional for one minute, but I have been put in unprofessional jobs for over a year. I am leaving the country. I don't care, just give me my money," and I hung up on the Matador bitch.

Maybe Matador will learn to take better care of their temps. They ignored me for over a year. I came to this country for an adventure, not to cry in a cubicle. Have fun taking hundreds of koalas off my cubicle walls; I'm going to Scotland to marry the son of a knight in a castle.

210

ABOUT THE AUTHOR

Jamie Baywood grew up in Petaluma, California. In 2010, she made the most impulsive decision of her life by moving to New Zealand. Getting Rooted in New Zealand is her first book about her experiences living there. Jamie is now married and living happily ever after in the United Kingdom. She is working on her second book.

Printed in Great Britain
by Amazon.co.uk, Ltd.,
Marston Gate.